easy low-carb

easy low-carb

RYLAND
PETERS
& SMALL

LONDON NEW YORK

First published in Great Britain in 2006
by Ryland Peters & Small
20–21 Jockey's Fields
London WC1R 4BW
www.rylandpeters.com
10 9 8 7 6 5 4 3 2 1

Introduction © Nicola Graimes 2006
Recipes © Maxine Clark, Clare Ferguson, Manisha Gambhir
Harkins, Jane Noraika, Elsa Petersen-Schepelern, Louise
Pickford, Jennie Shapter, Sonia Stevenson, Linda Tubby
and Laura Washburn, 2006
Design and photographs © Ryland Peters & Small 2006

ISBN-10: 1 84597 101 9
ISBN-13: 978 1 84597 101 4

A CIP catalogue record for this book is available from the
British Library.

Printed in China

Notes
• All spoon measurements are level unless otherwise specified.
• Eggs are medium unless otherwise specified. Recipes
containing raw or partially cooked egg, or raw fish or shellfish,
should not be served to the very young or old, those with
compromised immune systems or pregnant women.

Designers Catherine Griffin and Carl Hodson
Commissioning Editor Elsa Petersen-Schepelern
Editor Rachel Lawrence
Production Gavin Bradshaw
Picture Research Emily Westlake
Art Director Anne-Marie Bulat
Editorial Director Julia Charles

Index Penelope Kent

contents

introduction

It's tempting when eager to lose a few pounds to simply skip meals, but this can often have the reverse effect. This book encourages you to eat regular meals based on the main food groups – unrefined carbohydrates, protein, unsaturated fats, fruit and plenty of vegetables. By helping you to reduce food cravings, optimize metabolic rate (at which calories are burnt) and control appetite, this consequently leads to better weight control.

A low-carb diet provides a nutritious and varied alternative to a typical modern diet based on processed foods. Such foods are inherently high in refined carbohydrates, saturated or hydrogenated fats, sugar and additives, and are lacking in vital nutrients.

Low-carb diets are based on the basic principle of limiting carbohydrate intake rather than laborious calorie counting. That said, there are many different types of low-carb diets, including some which severely restrict the amount of carbohydrates eaten by ignoring certain food groups, including fruit and vegetables.

However, a low-carb diet doesn't have to mean limiting yourself to high protein foods and cutting out all sources of carbohydrate. With these recipes you can maintain a balanced diet without missing out on vital nutrients. A moderate intake of 'good' carbohydrates coupled with foods that have a low glycaemic index (see opposite) all have a part to play in sustainable weight loss.

Insulin levels

Controlling insulin levels in the body is the key to a low-carb diet. Insulin is a hormone secreted by the pancreas that is stimulated primarily by carbohydrate intake. Insulin is essential for good health since it plays a major role in converting carbohydrates into energy to be used by the body. It regulates the amount of glucose (sugar) in the bloodstream, removing any excess and storing it as fat. It also acts as the guardian of the body's fat reserves.

But that's not the complete picture: it's also possible to become insulin resistant. This means the body makes more and more insulin to cope with a continued excess of carbohydrates in the diet. The the body then becomes less responsive to the excessive amounts of the hormone present and produces even more insulin – and the cycle continues. Weight gain, diabetes, high blood pressure, heart disease, arthritis and kidney failure are all possible adverse effects of over-production of insulin. The only answer is to lower carbohydrate intake and cut back on high-GI foods in order to control insulin production and its negative effects.

Glycaemic Index

As well as being low-carb, many of the recipes in this book also have a low GI (glycaemic index) rating. The glycaemic index ranks any carbohydrate food from 0 to 100, based on how quickly it is broken down by the body and its subsequent effect on blood sugar levels. Meat, fish, shellfish, poultry, eggs, nuts, cheese and olive oil contain virtually no carbohydrates and therefore don't have a GI rating.

The lower a food's GI rating, the longer is takes for it to be digested and the smaller the rise in blood sugar levels and insulin response. In other words, low GI foods keep the body feeling full and produce a steady supply of energy. Foods with a high GI value have a more dramatic effect on blood sugar levels and trigger a quick release of insulin into the bloodstream. This leads to fluctuating energy levels, food cravings and mood swings.

However, there are some surprises in the glycaemic index. Wholemeal bread, for example, has a relatively high GI of 69, while multigrain has a medium GI of 55, which means that while they contain similar proportions of carbohydrates, they have different rates of absorption. Similarly, boiled new potatoes have a medium GI, while baked potatoes are high.

The GI value of carbohydrate foods is also influenced by protein and fat – either within the food or eaten with it. This acts as a brake on how quickly they are digested. Many foods are a combination of food groups: pulses, for instance, are a combination of carbohydrate and protein.

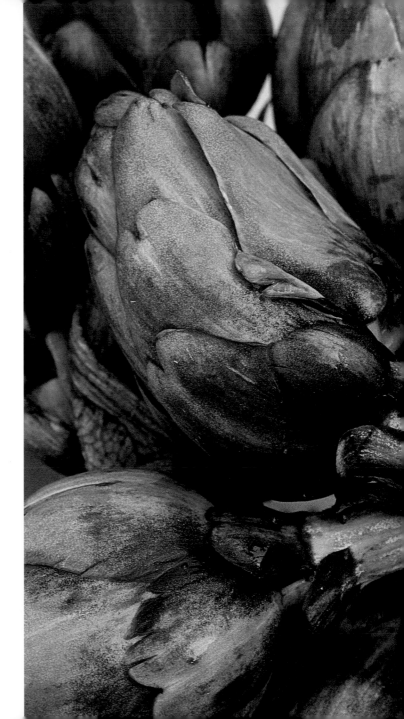

By contrast, unrefined carbohydrates (brown rice, wholegrain bread, pulses, wholemeal pasta, vegetables and fruit) provide valuable vitamins, minerals and fibre. That said, all carbohydrates influence blood sugar and insulin levels to a varying degree, which is why moderation is the key. By eating these foods in controlled amounts – one slice of bread, not two; or a small bowl of rice not a large plateful – on a daily basis you'll keep energy levels on an even keel and keep hunger pangs at bay, thereby avoiding the temptation to binge on unhealthy snacks.

Protein foods

Protein foods make you feel more alert and satisfy the appetite for longer than carbohydrate foods as they take longer to digest. This is the key to regulating blood sugar levels. Protein is found in both animal and plant foods. Certain protein foods are also high in saturated fats, such as red meat and dairy foods, so are best eaten in moderation. The preferred sources of protein are skinless poultry, lean meat, low-fat dairy, seafood, eggs, beans, lentils and soya-based foods, such as tofu.

Good and bad fats

Fat is often quoted as the dietary villain, yet just as there are 'good' and 'bad' carbohydrates, there are 'good' and 'bad' fats. Hydrogenated (trans) and saturated fats are the bad guys. The former are vegetable oils that have been heat-treated to turn them into solid fat and are often found in processed foods such as margarines, pies and snacks. Saturated fats tend to come from animal sources and

GI RATINGS

70 +	High GI
55–69	Medium GI
55 –	Low GI

The low-down on carbohydrates

It's important to remember that carbohydrates form an essential part of our diet and are a primary source of energy. However, there are different types of carbohydrate, some of which are nutritionally redundant. These are the refined types (see opposite page), which are stripped of vitamins minerals and fibre during processing. Refined carbohydrates have a significant impact on blood sugar and insulin levels, leading to yo-yoing energy levels, hunger pangs, cravings for more carbohydrates, and weight gain.

are found in cheese, butter and fatty meats. Good fats include the polyunsaturated and monounsaturated types. Plant-based fats such as olive oil, omega-3 fatty acids found in oily fish and flaxseeds, and omega-6 fatty acids, found in nuts and seeds are the preferred types.

Low-carb drinks

Water is the preferred drink of choice in a low-carb diet. Many of us don't drink enough water yet dehydration affects our ability to transport essential nutrients throughout the body. It also helps the body to flush out waste and toxins, aids concentration and improves energy levels. It is also naturally filling!

Fruit juices, such as orange or apple juice, are often high in carbohydrate and should be consumed in moderation. Berry-based juices are a better option and diluting fruit juice with mineral water is a good way of reducing the carbohydrate content.

Caffeine can affect the balance of insulin and blood sugar in the diet. Coffee contains more caffeine than tea and is best restricted to one cup a day at breakfast time and not on an empty stomach. Tea, particularly green and white tea, are high in antioxidants but again are best drunk in moderate amounts. Better still, opt for herbal teas, of which there are plenty of different flavours to choose from. Low-fat milks provide a protein boost and are also a low GI food.

Alcohol is high in sugar and has a high GI rating. It metabolizes quickly in the body, creating a short-term sugar high.

Having said that, there is nothing wrong with the occasional glass of wine or beer.

The recipes

The recipes in this book demonstrate that low-carb meals don't have to be dull or worthy. They take their inspiration from the many cuisines of the world, including Italian, French, Chinese, Indian and Thai. There is also a collection of vegetarian recipes and great ideas for desserts and party foods, too.

Each person's tolerance to carbohydrates is different, which is why at the end of each recipe you'll find a carbohydrate count (in grams), per serving. This enables you to plan your meals according to your dietary needs, depending on whether you want to lose weight or maintain a healthy weight level.

The easy-to-follow, delicious recipes can easily be adapted to suit even those not following a low-carb diet by serving them with traditional accompaniments such as potatoes or rice, for example.

Refined carbs to avoid:

White bread

White pasta and rice

Sugar and honey

Biscuits and cakes

Chocolates and sweets

Crisps

Sugary breakfast cereals and cereal bars

Ready-made sauces and gravy mixes

Pizzas

Pies and pastry

Pre-prepared meals

Fizzy drinks, cordials and juice drinks

snacks and party food

roasted and spiced nuts

your choice of freshly ground or crushed spices, such as:

cinnamon sticks

cardamom

nutmeg

mild chilli flakes

sesame seeds

cumin seeds

paprika

ginger

black pepper

grated citrus zest

Thai 7-spice

Japanese 7-spice

your choice of fresh, raw nuts, about 30 g or 4 tablespoons per person, such as:

peanuts

cashews

macadamias

almonds

pecans

1 tablespoon sunflower oil, for toasting (optional)

sea salt

small paper cups

serves 8

carbohydrate 3 g

Nuts are very nutritious and have virtually no carbohydrates, so they make a great alternative to high-carb snacks such as crisps. And while they are high in fat, it is the good unsaturated type. You can buy roasted nuts, but it's easy to roast your own, and you can add all sorts of delicious spices. Serve up to three kinds of nuts, but serve each kind separately.

The number one rule is fresh nuts and freshly ground spices. If using cinnamon sticks, break them up and grind to a powder in a coffee grinder or with a mortar and pestle.

Wipe out the grinder, then grind the black seeds from the green cardamom pods, if using (or buy them already podded – if you do it yourself, the seeds can be a little sticky). If using nutmeg, grate whole ones with a nutmeg grater, or on the finest side of a box grater.

To roast the nuts, heat a dry frying pan, add one kind of nut and cook, shaking the pan, until they're aromatic and slightly golden. You must stay with them, and keep shaking, or they will burn and be spoiled.

When ready, tip them into a wide, shallow bowl, then sprinkle with salt and one of the spices or citrus zest.

If preferred, you can cook the nuts with 1 tablespoon of sunflower oil, but your guests will love the flavour of dry-fried nuts and thank you for saving them from that tiny extra drop of oil.

To serve, drop about 2 tablespoons of the nuts into each paper cup, tiny china bowl or folded mini box, arrange on a tray and serve.

cucumber canapés

These are a great vegetarian canapé, but meat-eaters will love them too. As well as being low-carb, peas and cucumbers score well on the GI scale. You can add extra flavour with a few tablespoons of freshly grated Parmesan or other hard cheese. Pea omelette makes a tasty breakfast treat, too – divide the omelette mixture to make three separate omelettes.

1 long cucumber, about 4 cm diameter, sliced 5–10 mm thick

a large bunch of mint

sesame oil, to serve

pea omelette

175 g shelled green peas, fresh or frozen

6 eggs

butter or olive oil, for frying

sea salt and freshly ground black pepper

makes about 40

carbohydrate 1 g

To make the omelette, microwave the peas on HIGH for 2 minutes, or steam for 3 minutes until tender. Beat the eggs in a bowl with salt and pepper and a few tablespoons of cold water.

Heat a large heavy or non-stick frying pan, add oil or butter and heat for 1–2 minutes. Distribute half the peas evenly over the surface, then quickly pour in half the egg mixture until all the surface is just covered. Cook just until the omelette has set, then slide out onto a large flat plate and let cool. Repeat with the remaining peas and egg mixture.

Slice the omelettes into squares a little smaller than the cucumber rounds (or cut out rounds with the top of a small glass). Arrange the cucumber slices on a serving tray, top each one with a piece of pea omelette, a mint leaf and a drop of sesame oil, then serve.

These leaf scoops are tasty and refreshing without being too filling. Use small crisp leaves with a good shape instead of bread or toast as the basis for party canapés or lunchtime bruschetta. Lengths of celery or segments of fennel would also work well as scoops. When choosing your fillings, bear in mind what the next course will be.

leaf scoop fillings

125 g soft goats' cheese

16 crisp salad leaves, such as chicory, Little Gem or baby radicchio

2 tablespoons salmon or trout caviar

4 tablespoons Baba Ganoush (page 19)

1 teaspoon chopped fresh parsley

1 teaspoon toasted sesame seeds (page 52)

freshly ground black pepper

lemon zest, to garnish

makes 16

carbohydrate 1 g

Divide the goats' cheese into 8 small balls and place each one on a leaf. Place a small dollop of caviar next to each of the goats' cheese balls, then sprinkle with black pepper and decorate with lemon zest.

Take the remaining leaves and put half a tablespoon of baba ganoush in each one. Sprinkle with parsley and sesame seeds.

Variations Alternative low-carb fillings include smoked chicken with salsa, soft goats' cheese mixed with chopped herbs and smoked salmon and crème fraîche. Alternatively, sauté some onion and garlic in butter or olive oil until almost melted, then mix with ricotta.

Baba ganoush is the famous creamy aubergine purée with smoky overtones. To achieve the authentic smoky flavour, it's best to char the aubergines over a barbecue, or under a hot grill or over an open flame on a gas stove. Serve baba ganoush as a dip for parties, in Leaf Scoop Fillings (page 16) or with other dishes as a first course.

baba ganoush

3 aubergines

4 tablespoons natural yoghurt

2 tablespoons tahini paste

1 garlic clove, crushed

1 teaspoon sea salt

freshly squeezed juice of 1–2 lemons, to taste

1 tablespoon chopped fresh flat leaf parsley (optional)

crudités, such as lettuce, cucumber or courgette, to serve

serves 8

carbohydrate 4 g

Put the aubergines on top of the open gas flame on top of the stove and cook until well charred on all sides. The steam created inside the vegetable will cook the flesh. The aubergines must be charred all over and soft in the middle. Remove from the flame and let cool on a plate.

When cool, carefully pull off the skins and stems. Don't leave any charred bits. Put the flesh into a bowl, then blend with a hand-held stick blender or potato masher: the texture should not be too smooth. Add the yoghurt, tahini, garlic and salt and blend again.

Add the juice of 1 lemon, taste, then gradually add more juice until you achieve flavour and texture to your taste. Transfer to a serving bowl and sprinkle with finely chopped parsley, if using. Serve with a selection of crudités.

red pepper roulade

2 large red peppers

150 g fresh mozzarella cheese

8 large fresh basil leaves

1 tablespoon pesto (page 95)

extra virgin olive oil

lemon-marinated courgette

3 medium courgettes

4 tablespoons olive oil, plus extra for brushing

2 tablespoons freshly squeezed lemon juice

1 tablespoon freshly grated Parmesan cheese

2 anchovies, rinsed and finely chopped

aubergine, salami and artichoke

1 medium aubergine

4 tablespoons olive oil, plus extra for brushing

8 thin slices salami

4 artichokes marinated in oil, drained and halved

2 tablespoons freshly squeezed lemon juice

1 tablespoon capers, rinsed, drained and chopped

sea salt and freshly ground black pepper

cocktail sticks

a ridged stove-top grill pan

serves 4

carbohydrate 9 g

These Italian-style marinated vegetables look impressive and are a good alternative to high-carb starters such as garlic bread or bruschetta. Marinating the ingredients first gives them extra flavour and cooking the vegetables on a ridged grill pan gives them an attractive striped pattern.

three marinated antipasti

To make the red pepper roulades, char-grill the peppers until soft and black. Rinse off the charred skin, cut the peppers in quarters lengthways, cut off the stalks and scrape out the seeds. Cut the mozzarella into 8 thin slices. Put a slice inside each pepper strip, put a basil leaf on top and season well with salt and pepper. Roll up from one end and secure with a cocktail stick. Put the pesto in a bowl and beat in enough olive oil to thin it to pouring consistency. Add the rolls and toss to coat. Cover and let marinate for at least 2 hours.

To make the lemon-marinated courgette, heat a ridged stove-top grill pan until hot. Cut the courgettes into long thin slices, brush with olive oil and cook for 2–3 minutes on each side. Transfer to a shallow dish. Put the 4 tablespoons olive oil, lemon juice, Parmesan and anchovies in a bowl, beat with a fork, then pour over the courgettes. Cover and let marinate as above.

To make the aubergine antipasto, cut the aubergine into 8 thin slices, brush lightly with olive oil and cook on the same grill pan for 2–3 minutes on each side. Put a slice of salami on each one, then an artichoke half at one side. Fold the aubergine in half to cover the artichoke, secure with a cocktail stick and put in a shallow dish. Put the 4 tablespoons olive oil in a bowl, whisk in the lemon juice, capers, salt and pepper, then spoon over the aubergines. Cover and let marinate as above. Serve all three recipes on a serving dish as mixed antipasti.

Here is a simple, delicious snack, with mellow olive oil accentuating the flavours. It's traditional to sprinkle the aubergine slices with salt to extract moisture before cooking. In the past this also extracted bitterness, but modern hothouse varieties of aubergine are no longer as bitter.

aubergine antipasto
with pine nuts and herbs

2–3 medium aubergines, about 750 g

2 tablespoons sea salt flakes

1 tablespoon extra virgin olive oil, plus extra for brushing

50 g pine nuts

1 small bunch of fresh mint, half chopped, half in sprigs

1 small bunch of fresh flat leaf parsley, half chopped, half in sprigs

2 tablespoons aged balsamic vinegar

freshly ground black pepper

a ridged stove-top grill pan

serves 4–6

carbohydrate 5 g

Cut the aubergines lengthways into 1 cm slices. Score both sides of each slice with a fork. Sprinkle with salt, drain in a colander for 20 minutes, then pat dry with kitchen paper.

Meanwhile heat a ridged stove-top grill pan until very hot. Wipe with olive oil using a wad of crumpled kitchen paper or a heatproof brush. Brush each slice of aubergine with olive oil. Arrange on the hot pan, pressing down firmly. Cook for 3–5 minutes each side until grill-marked, tender and aromatic. Heat 1 tablespoon olive oil in a frying pan, add the pine nuts and toast gently until golden. Set aside.

Scatter the cooked aubergine with chopped mint, chopped parsley, black pepper and a few drops of balsamic vinegar. Loop the slices on serving plates, add the pine nuts and sprigs of mint and parsley and serve.

Piquillo peppers are vividly red, mildly spicy-hot and are often sold roasted and peeled in cans and jars. Buy them from Spanish stores and good delis. This is an easy snack food and can be ready in under 10 minutes. Serve hot or cold with baby salad greens.

spanish stuffed peppers

185 g canned peeled piquillo peppers or pimientos

4 tablespoons olive oil

3–4 garlic cloves, chopped

400 g canned white beans, such as cannellini or butter beans, part-drained (reserve the liquid)

2 tablespoons sherry vinegar

a handful of fresh thyme or mint, chopped

a handful of baby salad leaves such as spinach or watercress, or flat leaf parsley

sea salt and freshly ground black pepper

serves 4

carbohydrate 16 g

Drain the piquillo peppers, reserving the liquid. Pat dry with kitchen paper.

Heat the oil, garlic and white beans in a non-stick frying pan and mash with a fork to a thick, coarse purée. Add 1 tablespoon of the sherry vinegar and 1 tablespoon of bean liquid, stir, then season well with salt and pepper. Let cool slightly, then stuff each piquillo with the mixture and sprinkle with the thyme.

Cut each piquillo into thick slices or leave whole. Serve on 4 plates, adding some salad leaves to each. Trickle over a tablespoon of the preserving liquid and the remaining vinegar before serving.

Variation Instead of canned piquillos or pimientos, use 4 red peppers, halved lengthways and deseeded. Grill them skin side up until blistered. Rub off the skins, stuff with the mixture, roll up, then serve as in the main recipe.

Little bistros in French seaside villages often serve dishes such as the legendary garlic prawns. Prawns and olive oil are virtually no-carb and this dish makes an ideal starter for garlic lovers – the parsley is said to help with its after-effects. When buying fresh prawns look for firm bodies and avoid any that are limp or sticky.

garlic prawns

125 ml olive oil

1 kg raw prawn tails, shell on

8–10 garlic cloves, chopped

a large handful of flat-leaf parsley, chopped

coarse sea salt and freshly ground black pepper

lemon wedges, to serve

serves 4

carbohydrate 2 g

Heat the oil in a large sauté pan. When hot but not smoking, add the prawns and garlic and cook until the prawns turn pink, 3–5 minutes. Be careful not to let the garlic burn. Remove from the heat, sprinkle with salt, pepper and parsley and mix well. Serve immediately with lemon wedges.

Variation Spanish Garlic Prawns At the same time as the salt and pepper, add the juice of ½ lemon, a few tablespoons dry sherry, a pinch of smoked hot paprika and a pinch of dried chilli flakes.

ice-cold prairie oysters

Prairie Oysters are usually regarded as a hangover cure, but take away their medicinal nature, and replace the egg yolk with a real oyster, and they are utterly delicious. Serve this as a one-off canapé-cum-cocktail when people first arrive. Make sure all the ingredients are ice-cold, and the vodka has been in the freezer.

600 ml tomato juice

200 ml ice-cold vodka

freshly squeezed juice of 6 limes or 2 large lemons

a dash of Tabasco, or to taste

crushed ice

12 freshly shucked oysters

sprigs of fresh mint (optional)

sea salt and freshly ground black pepper

mini wedges or thin slices of lime, to serve

cocktail sticks

serves 12

carbohydrate 2 g

Put the tomato juice, vodka, lime or lemon juice and Tabasco in a jug half-full of crushed ice. Stir well. (If making in advance, omit the ice and chill well.)

Put 1 oyster in each of 12 shot, aquavit or sherry glasses, add the chilled vodka mixture, then top with a mint leaf, a little salt and pepper and a lime wedge or slice speared with a cocktail stick. Use any leftover Bloody Mary mixture for people who don't like oysters.

Variation Before you start, rub a lemon wedge around the rim of each glass, and press the rim into a saucer of salt, just as if you were making a Margarita.

2 spicy uncooked
chorizo sausages

1 tablespoon extra
virgin olive oil

20 freshly shucked oysters

shallot vinegar

3 tablespoons
red wine vinegar

2 tablespoons finely
chopped shallot

1 tablespoon snipped
fresh chives

sea salt and freshly
ground black pepper

cocktail sticks

*a large platter filled with a layer of
ice cubes*

serves 4

carbohydrate 3 g

The combination may sound slightly unusual, but it is, in fact, totally delicious. Fresh oysters eaten with a nibble of the hot sausage is a taste sensation – try it, you'll be amazed.

oysters
with spicy chorizo

To make the shallot vinegar, put the ingredients into a bowl and mix well. Pour into a small dish and set aside until required.

Cut the chorizo into bite-size pieces. Heat the olive oil in a non-stick frying pan and fry for 1 minutes on each side, then let cool slightly. Alternatively, preheat a barbecue and cook the sausages whole for 8–10 minutes, then cut them into bite-size pieces.

Spike the chorizo pieces onto cocktail sticks and arrange them in the centre of a large serving platter filled with ice. Put the oysters into their half-shells and arrange on the ice. Serve with the shallot vinegar.

Chorizo, a paprika-rich, spicy Spanish sausage, is smoky and garlicky and can be bought in links or in long, curved shapes, raw or cooked. This recipe needs the raw, spicy chorizo sold in links; you'll find it in specialist delicatessens or Spanish grocers. Serve with cocktail sticks for dunking the sausage in the juices.

chorizo in red wine

750 g uncooked chorizo sausage, or other dense, garlic-flavoured pork sausage

2 tablespoons extra virgin olive oil

150 ml red Rioja wine

4 sprigs of thyme (optional)

freshly ground black pepper

cocktail sticks

serves 4

carbohydrate 6 g

Cut the chorizo into 1 cm chunks. Heat half the oil in a large, non-stick frying pan until very hot. Add half the chorizo and fry on both sides for 1 minute each. Remove with a slotted spoon and keep hot. Add the remaining oil and remaining chorizo. Cook and remove as before.

Add the wine and thyme, if using, to the pan and swirl to dissolve the sediment. Cook gently to thicken and reduce the sauce. Pour the sauce over the hot chorizo, sprinkle with pepper and serve with cocktail sticks.

Note If chorizo is difficult to find, use cooked, garlicky Polish pork sausage (kielbasa) and add 2 teaspoons of paprika to the juices in the pan.

600 g deep-fried tofu

150 g thick natural yoghurt

2 tablespoons tomato purée

1 garlic clove, crushed

3 cm fresh ginger*, grated

1 green chilli, finely chopped, including seeds

1 teaspoon sea salt

1 teaspoon cumin seeds, lightly toasted in a dry frying pan and ground in a spice or coffee grinder

2 teaspoons coriander seeds, lightly toasted in a dry frying pan and ground in a spice or coffee grinder

freshly squeezed juice of ½ lemon

to serve

fresh coriander, coarsely chopped (optional)

mini lemon wedges

a baking tray

cocktail sticks

makes about 12

carbohydrate 2 g

These succulent, spicy morsels are original enough to surprise any guest, but be sure to make plenty of them since they are very moreish. They make an ideal canapé to serve with cocktails. Tofu absorbs flavours very well – to be super-organized, marinate it overnight in the fridge.

tandoori tofu

Cut the tofu into bite-sized pieces and put into a large bowl.

Put the yoghurt into another bowl, add the tomato purée, garlic, ginger, chilli, salt and toasted cumin and coriander seeds, and stir well. Spoon the mixture over the tofu and toss gently so that each piece is well coated. Set aside to marinate in the refrigerator for at least 1 hour.

Spread over a baking tray and cook in a preheated oven at 200°C (400°F) Gas 6 for 40 minutes, stirring halfway through the cooking time.

Transfer to a platter, then sprinkle with the lemon juice and coriander, if using.

Let your guests help themselves to these succulent pieces of tofu, using a cocktail stick. Alternatively, thread a tiny wedge of lemon onto each stick, followed by a tofu cube.

*Note The best way to store fresh ginger is in the freezer. Using a fine grater, grate as much of the frozen ginger as you need with no peeling or waste.

smoked salmon omelette

It is important to start folding the omelette while it is still slightly liquid in the centre to avoid it over-cooking and becoming tough and leathery. Make sure the person who is going to eat it is ready first, rather than the omelette.

75 g smoked salmon, cut into thin strips

1 tablespoon milk

3 large eggs

2 teaspoons unsalted butter

2 tablespoons crème fraîche

1 tablespoon chopped fresh dill

sea salt and freshly ground black pepper

an 18-cm heavy omelette pan

serves 1

carbohydrate 2 g

Put half the smoked salmon in a bowl, add the milk and let stand for 15 minutes.

Break the eggs into a bowl whisk briefly with a fork, just enough to mix the yolks and whites. Season with salt and plenty of pepper, then stir in the milk and smoked salmon.

Heat the butter in the omelette pan. When the butter starts to foam, pour in the egg mixture and cook over medium-high heat, drawing the mixture from the sides to the centre as it sets. Let the liquid flow and fill the space at the sides.

After a short time, the omelette will be cooked but still creamy in the centre. Top the omelette with the crème fraîche and sprinkle with chopped dill and the remaining smoked salmon.

Fold over a third of the omelette to the centre, then fold over the remaining third, slide onto a warmed plate and serve immediately.

Dried porcini are a very useful ingredient to have in your store cupboard. They are one of the best mushrooms, with an intense, rich flavour that will pervade the omelette. Strain the soaking liquid from the porcini and add a spoonful to the omelette mixture, or keep it for a soup or stew.

porcini frittata

15 g dried porcini mushrooms

6 eggs

3 tablespoons mascarpone cheese

3 tablespoons chopped fresh flat leaf parsley

3 tablespoons extra virgin olive or sunflower oil

1 onion, halved and sliced

125 g button mushrooms, sliced

1 tablespoon freshly grated Parmesan cheese

1 tablespoon unsalted butter

75 g fresh wild mushrooms

sea salt and freshly ground black pepper

a 20-cm heavy non-stick frying pan

serves 2–3

carbohydrate 13 g

Put the porcini in a small bowl and cover with warm water. Let soak for 30 minutes. Break 1 of the eggs into a bowl, add the mascarpone and mix well. Add the remaining eggs and whisk briefly with a fork. Stir in the parsley and season with salt and pepper.

Heat 1 tablespoon of the oil in the frying pan, add the onion and cook over low heat until soft. Add another tablespoon of oil and the mushrooms and cook for 5 minutes. Drain the porcini and chop if large. Add to the pan and cook for 2 minutes.

Using a slotted spoon, transfer the mushrooms and onions to the eggs and mix gently.

Wipe out the frying pan with kitchen paper, add the remaining oil and heat gently. Add the frittata mixture and cook over low heat until browned on the underside and nearly set on top. Sprinkle with Parmesan and place under a preheated grill to finish cooking the top and melt the cheese. Transfer to a warm serving plate.

Melt the butter in the frying pan, add the wild mushrooms and sauté quickly. Spoon the mushrooms over the top of the frittata and serve.

piperrada

Versions of this handsome, delicious dish are found all over Spain and the South of France. Ingredients and cooking methods vary from region to region, but peppers, garlic, tomatoes, ham and often eggs are essentials, as is fruity, robust olive oil. It makes a great informal first course, served straight from the pan.

4 tablespoons extra virgin olive oil

1 Spanish onion, sliced into rings

3 garlic cloves, sliced

2 red peppers, halved, deseeded and sliced

2 yellow peppers, halved, deseeded and sliced

2 ripe red tomatoes, skinned and sliced

6 eggs

4 slices serrano or Parma ham

1 dried red chilli, crumbled (optional)

sea salt and freshly ground black pepper

serves 6–8

carbohydrate 10 g

Heat 3 tablespoons of the oil in a heavy-based frying pan over a medium heat. Add the onion and garlic and sauté until soft and fragrant but not browned. Add the peppers and tomatoes. Cover the pan, reduce the heat and cook to form a soft thick purée, about 8–12 minutes. Season to taste.

Break the eggs into a bowl, season with salt and pepper and stir with a fork. Using a spatula, push a space clear near the centre of the pan. Add the remaining oil to the space, then pour in the eggs. Stir gently over medium heat until semi-set. Turn off the heat.

Fold the slices of ham into rosettes or pleats, then add to the pan. Sprinkle over some dried chilli, if using, and serve straight from the pan.

salads

750 g ripe vine tomatoes

1 large shallot, or 1 small red onion, thinly sliced

sea salt and freshly ground black pepper

anchovy vinaigrette

1 garlic clove

½ teaspoon Dijon mustard

2 tablespoons white wine vinegar

6 anchovy fillets, packed in oil

120 ml extra virgin olive oil

a small handful of basil leaves

freshly ground black pepper

to serve

a handful of flat leaf parsley, finely chopped

a few basil leaves, torn

serves 4

carbohydrate 7 g

Tomatoes are rich in antioxidants – try to buy them when they are very ripe and full of flavour. Here they are dressed with a vinaigrette infused with the distinctive flavour of anchovies. The anchovy vinaigrette also makes a tasty dip for crudités.

tomato salad
with anchovy vinaigrette

To make the vinaigrette, put the garlic, mustard, vinegar and anchovies in a small food processor and blend well. Add the oil, 1 tablespoon at a time, then blend in the basil. Season with pepper and set aside.

Cut the tomatoes into 4–8 wedges, depending on their size. Arrange on a plate and sprinkle with the shallot or onion. Season lightly with salt, then spoon the dressing over the top. Sprinkle with the parsley, basil and pepper, and serve at room temperature.

Breathtakingly simple, but gorgeous in taste, this salsa is fabulous with these little lamb cutlets. The roasted tomatoes simply melt in the mouth and make an excellent accompaniment for meat, fish or poultry. Spoon the salsa into a small bowl on the plate, with the cutlets beside.

roasted tomato and oregano salsa
with lamb cutlets

12 plum tomatoes, about 4 cm diameter

4 sprigs of oregano

5 tablespoons extra virgin olive oil

2 garlic cloves, thinly sliced

2 tablespoons balsamic vinegar

a pinch of sea salt flakes, crushed

1 teaspoon harissa paste or a dash of Tabasco sauce

1 tablespoon freshly ground black pepper

lamb cutlets

olive oil, for frying

12 lamb cutlets, frenched and chined, then all fat removed

sea salt and freshly ground black pepper

a few oregano leaves, to serve

a cocktail stick

serves 4

carbohydrate 8 g

Prick the tomatoes once each with a cocktail stick. Put the tomatoes and oregano in a plastic bag with 2 tablespoons of the olive oil and the garlic. Shake to coat with oil, then transfer to a roasting tin and roast in a preheated oven at 200°C (400°F) Gas 6 until half collapsed, with the tomato skins split and slightly browned, 15–30 minutes, depending on the size of the tomatoes. Brown under the grill if necessary.

To make the dressing, put the balsamic vinegar in a bowl, add the remaining olive oil, the salt and harissa or Tabasco and beat with a fork. Put the tomatoes in small serving bowls, pour over the dressing and sprinkle with the pepper. Keep them warm in the turned-off oven while you fry the cutlets.

To cook the cutlets, put the oil in a frying pan, heat well, then add the cutlets, in batches if necessary, and sprinkle with salt. Fry at a high heat for about 1–2 minutes on each side until browned but still pink in the middle. Divide the cutlets among 4 heated dinner plates and add the small bowls of tomatoes. Sprinkle with oregano, salt and black pepper. Serve with small spoons to eat the tomatoes.

tomato salads

Tomato salads appear in infinite variety. At their best they are good, ripe, sliced tomatoes sprinkled just with vinegar, salt and pepper, but no oil. The salt brings out the tomato juices, which help form the dressing. For something a little more exotic, make a Moroccan vinaigrette to toss the tomatoes in. Look out for unusual varieties of tomato.

4 large, ripe tomatoes, sliced, or 500 g mixed red and yellow cherry tomatoes, halved

tomato farmer's salad

3–4 tablespoons white wine vinegar

sea salt and freshly ground black pepper

carbohydrate 5 g

Put the sliced tomatoes on a plate or in a bowl. Sprinkle with vinegar, salt and pepper and set aside for a few minutes until ready to serve.

tomato and onion salad

1 red onion, halved and thinly sliced, or 6 spring onions, thinly sliced diagonally

3–4 tablespoons white wine vinegar

sea salt and freshly ground black pepper

carbohydrate 5 g

Put the onion in a bowl, separating the half-rings as you do so. Add the tomatoes to the bowl. Sprinkle with vinegar, salt and pepper and set aside for a few minutes until ready to serve. Turn gently before serving.

moroccan tomato salad with preserved lemon and harissa vinaigrette (opposite)

moroccan tomato salad with preserved lemon and harissa vinaigrette

1–2 preserved lemons

6 tablespoons extra virgin olive oil

1 tablespoon white wine vinegar

1 teaspoon harissa paste

2 spring onions, chopped

1 tablespoon chopped fresh mint, plus a handful of leaves, to serve

carbohydrate 5 g

serves 4

To prepare the preserved lemons, cut them in quarters, scrape out and discard the flesh and cut the skin into strips. Mix the oil, vinegar and harissa paste in a large bowl then add the tomatoes, lemon strips and spring onions. Mix gently, then toss in the mint. Set aside for a few minutes for the flavours to develop, then serve with mint leaves on top.

Note Preserved lemons are available in North African and French delicatessens. If unavailable, use the grated zest of 2 unwaxed lemons.

Vegetables taste wonderful when grilled or cooked on the barbecue – it brings out their natural sweetness. Look out for the long, thin red peppers (ramiro or romano) when available – they are particularly good grilled.

salad of roasted peppers and asparagus

½ red onion, sliced

6 sweet red peppers, halved and deseeded

extra virgin olive oil, for brushing

500 g asparagus spears, trimmed

250 g mangetouts

75 g mixed salad leaves

a handful of fresh parsley and dill leaves

50 g hazelnuts, toasted in a dry frying pan and coarsely chopped

hazelnut oil dressing

4 tablespoons hazelnut oil

2 tablespoons extra virgin olive oil

1 tablespoon sherry vinegar

sea salt and freshly ground black pepper

a ridged stove-top grill pan

serves 4–6

carbohydrate 19 g

Put the onion in a sieve, sprinkle with salt and let drain over a bowl for 30 minutes. Rinse under cold running water and pat dry with kitchen paper.

Brush the peppers with olive oil and heat a ridged stove-top grill pan to hot. Add the peppers, skin side down, put a heavy weight, such as a saucepan, on top and cook until tender. Turn the pieces over and repeat the process. Alternatively, cook the peppers on a preheated barbecue for 15 minutes, turning frequently until charred all over.

Transfer the peppers to a plastic bag, seal and let soften until cool. Peel off the skin and discard the seeds, then cut the flesh into thick strips.

Brush the asparagus with olive oil and cook on a ridged stove-top grill pan or preheated barbecue for 2 minutes each side until charred and tender.

Put the mangetouts in a saucepan of lightly salted boiling water and boil for 1–2 minutes. Drain and refresh under cold running water.

Put the onion, peppers, asparagus and mangetouts in a large bowl and toss gently. Add the salad leaves, herbs and hazelnuts. Put the dressing ingredients in a bowl and whisk well. Pour over the salad, toss until coated and serve.

courgette, feta and mint salad

With the refreshing taste of fresh mint, this satisfying summer salad makes a superb accompaniment to grilled or barbecued poultry, meat or fish dishes, such as Char-grilled Spiced Prawns (page 117).

6 large courgettes

3 tablespoons extra virgin olive oil

150 g feta cheese, crumbled

a handful of fresh mint leaves

1 tablespoon toasted sesame seeds*

dressing

4 tablespoons extra virgin olive oil

1 tablespoon freshly squeezed lemon juice

1 small garlic clove, crushed

sea salt and freshly ground black pepper

a ridged stove-top grill pan

serves 4

carbohydrate 8 g

Cut the courgettes diagonally into thick slices, toss with the olive oil and season with salt and pepper. Heat a ridged stove-top grill pan or barbecue to hot. Cook the courgettes for 2 minutes each side, or until charred and tender. Remove and let cool.

Put all the dressing ingredients in a screw-top jar and shake well. Add salt and pepper to taste.

Put the courgettes, feta and mint in a large bowl, add the dressing and toss well until evenly coated. Sprinkle with the sesame seeds and serve at once.

*Note To toast sesame seeds, put them in a dry frying pan and toast gently over medium heat until golden and aromatic. Take care as they burn easily. Remove from the heat, let cool and set aside until required.

1 bag tatsoi or other small leaves, about 75 g

1 frisée (curly endive), leaves separated

½ tablespoon olive oil, for frying

6 thin slices smoked pancetta or bacon

1 ripe Hass avocado

dressing

6 tablespoons extra virgin olive oil

1 tablespoon sherry vinegar or rice vinegar

½ garlic clove, crushed

a few drops of balsamic vinegar

sea salt and freshly ground black pepper

serves 4

carbohydrate 2 g

Tatsoi is a crisp baby Chinese leaf sold in many supermarkets. It's like a mini bok choy leaf – you may find it in the stir-fry vegetable section. It's good in stir-fries, but even better as a salad leaf. If you can't find it, use watercress. The avocado should be scooped out with a teaspoon – when sliced it loses much of its appeal. This salad is delicious as a first course.

tatsoi, avocado and frisée
with pancetta

Wash the tatsoi and frisée leaves and dry in a salad spinner. Put in a plastic bag and chill.

Heat the olive oil in a frying pan, add the pancetta and cook at medium-high heat, without disturbing the pancetta, until crisp on one side. Using tongs, turn the slices over and fry until the other side is crisp. Remove and drain on kitchen paper, then cut into 5 cm lengths.

Put the dressing ingredients in a salad bowl and beat with a fork or small whisk. When ready to serve, add the leaves and turn in the dressing, using your hands. Cut the avocado in half and remove the stone. Using a teaspoon, scoop out balls of avocado into the salad. Add the crispy pancetta and serve.

about 12 mini asparagus tips

a handful of mini green beans, untrimmed

4 mini courgettes, cut into thirds lengthways (optional)

100 g sugar snap peas

100 g shelled green peas

100 g mini spring onions

75 g nuts such as hazelnuts or macadamias, toasted in a dry frying pan, then crushed into halves or big pieces, or pine nuts

sea salt and freshly ground black pepper

fresh Parmesan cheese, to serve (optional)

dressing

6 tablespoons extra virgin olive oil

1 tablespoon Japanese rice vinegar or white wine vinegar

½ teaspoon Dijon mustard

serves 4

carbohydrate 11 g

This is a great vegetarian salad – full of fresh flavours and quick and easy to make. Cook the vegetables ahead of time and leave to chill, then assemble the dish just before serving. Don't overcook the vegetables – they should retain some bite. Serve this as a salad in its own right, or to accompany a grilled steak, such as Rib Eye Steak with Anchovy Butter (page 164).

green vegetable salad

Microwave the asparagus tips, beans, courgettes, if using, sugar snaps and green peas separately on HIGH for 2 minutes each, then transfer immediately to a bowl of ice cubes and water. This stops them cooking and sets the colour. Alternatively, bring a large saucepan of water to the boil, then add each vegetable and blanch until just tender, but still al dente. Keep the peas until the end, and drain well before chilling.

To make the dressing, put the oil, vinegar and mustard in a salad bowl, season with salt and pepper and beat well with a fork or small whisk to form an emulsion. Add the drained vegetables, one kind at a time, and toss until lightly coated. Arrange the asparagus, beans, courgettes and spring onions on a serving platter or 4 plates. Add the sugar snaps and green peas, then sprinkle with the dressing and toasted nuts. Shave fresh Parmesan over the top, if using, and sprinkle with salt and pepper.

This colourful, fresh-tasting salsa is an excellent accompaniment for duck or pork, such as Spanish Duck with Olives (page 160) or Slow-roasted Pork Loin with Rosemary, Madeira and Orange (page 174). Chinese yard-long beans are good in salads because they keep their crunch, but use regular beans if these are hard to find.

green apple salsa

3 green peppers

2 Chinese yard-long beans, cut in 4, or 10 green beans

a 20-cm cucumber

1 white onion or a large handful of spring onions, sliced

freshly squeezed juice of 1½–2 oranges

2 Granny Smith apples, cored and diced

a large bunch of mint or basil, finely chopped (optional)

sea salt and freshly ground black pepper

serves 4

carbohydrate 15 g

Using a vegetable peeler, peel the peppers. Cut off the stalks and deseed. Cut into strips lengthways, then into dice, about ½ cm.

Top and tail the beans, then steam or microwave until cooked but still crisp. Plunge immediately in cold water and run the cold water until the beans are quite cool. Pat dry and cut into dice.

Cut the cucumber in half lengthways and scrape out the seed section. Cut the cucumber into strips, then into dice.

Put the peppers, beans, cucumber and onion in a bowl, squeeze over the orange juice, then sprinkle with salt and pepper. Set aside for at least 30 minutes to develop the flavour. Just before serving, add the diced apple and toss to coat with the juice. Sprinkle the mint or basil over the top, if using, then serve.

mozzarella, tomato and rocket salad

3 buffalo mozzarella cheeses, 150 g each

4 large, juicy, sun-ripened red tomatoes, thickly sliced

350 g fresh wild rocket

6–8 tablespoons good quality extra virgin olive oil

sea salt and freshly ground black pepper

black olives, to serve (optional)

serves 4

carbohydrate 6 g

The famous Italian caprese salad normally includes basil. In this variation, rocket adds a curious, peppery bite. Do use milky, soft buffalo mozzarella for its superb taste. Add red-ripe, flavourful tomatoes and a good-quality extra virgin olive oil and this dish becomes sublime. Never refrigerate it – make just a few minutes before eating.

Drain the mozzarellas. Slice thickly or pull them apart into big rough chunks, showing the grainy strands. Arrange down one side of a large serving platter.

Arrange the tomatoes in a second line down the middle of the plate. If they are very large, cut them in half first, then into semi-circles. Add the wild rocket leaves down the other side of the platter.

Sprinkle with salt and pepper, then just before serving trickle the olive oil over the top. Serve with black olives, if you like.

In this crispy salad the green herbs and beans are combined with the vivid colour of watermelon and the tangy bite of feta cheese for a delicious summer meal. Savory is a highly aromatic herb with a peppery, spicy flavour. There are two varieties – summer and winter – and both go well with beans, such as edamame. If you can't find it, use a handful of rocket instead.

savory feta salad
with sugar snap peas, edamame and watermelon

200 g edamame (fresh soya beans)
200 g broad beans, shelled
150 g sugar snap peas
½ small watermelon
4 tablespoons sunflower oil
200 g feta cheese
young leaves from 5 sprigs of savory
freshly ground black pepper

serves 6

carbohydrate 22 g

Bring a large saucepan of unsalted water to the boil. Add the edamame and broad beans and blanch for 2 minutes. Drain and refresh in cold water, then remove the edamame from their pods and the broad beans from their skins. Put in a large serving bowl.

Blanch the sugar snap peas in boiling salted water for 30 seconds, drain, refresh under cold running water, drain again, then slice lengthways. Add to the serving bowl with the edamame and broad beans.

Peel and slice the watermelon over a bowl to catch the juices. Cut the watermelon into small wedges, then add to the salad. Squeeze a few pieces to get about 3 tablespoons of juice in a separate bowl. Whisk the oil into the watermelon juice, then pour over the salad.

Crumble the feta over the top, sprinkle with young savory leaves and pepper, then serve.

250 g fresh ricotta cheese

4 eggs

1 egg yolk

20 g plain flour

50 g pecorino cheese, grated

½ teaspoon coarsely crushed dried green peppercorns

a small bunch of chives, with flowers if possible

a small bunch of chervil

a small bunch of tarragon

3 tomatoes, preferably an heirloom variety such as Green Zebra, cut into wedges, to serve

basil oil

6 tablespoons freshly chopped basil

150 ml extra virgin olive oil

a 500 g loaf tin, greased with butter

a roasting tin or similar dish, to hold the loaf tin

serves 6

carbohydrate 4 g

Make this delicately flavoured terrine in the summer with really fresh herbs. If chives are in flower, pluck the petals and sprinkle them on top. Serve with accompaniments, such as flavoursome organic tomatoes or locally grown varieties from specialist greengrocers or farmers' markets.

baked ricotta and herb terrine

Put the ricotta in a bowl and beat with a wooden spoon until smooth. Beat in the eggs and the extra egg yolk, one at a time. Put the flour, pecorino and green peppercorns in a bowl, stir well, then beat into the ricotta mixture.

Reserve a few chives, then coarsely chop the remaining chives, chervil and tarragon. Fold them into the ricotta. Spoon the mixture into the prepared loaf tin, stand it in a roasting tin and fill with enough water to come halfway up the outside of the loaf tin. Bake uncovered in a preheated oven at 180°C (350°F) Gas 4 for 35–45 minutes until risen, golden and set.

Meanwhile, to make the basil oil, put the basil and olive oil in a blender and blend until completely smooth – if not, pour through a fine strainer.

Remove the loaf tin from the roasting tin and let stand (as the terrine cools it will shrink away from the sides). After about 8 minutes, run a knife around the sides of the terrine, then carefully invert it onto a serving dish or board and cut into slices. Arrange the tomatoes around the terrine and sprinkle with the basil oil. Add the reserved whole chives and chive flowers, if available, and serve. If serving cold, let cool for at least 15 minutes.

In this summery salad the nuttiness of chickpeas is combined with roasted herby red peppers, parsley and shallot. Dry-frying the cumin enhances and mellows its flavour and when used in the vinaigrette it gives this salad a North African feel.

chickpea salad

250 g dried chickpeas

1 fresh bay leaf

2 red peppers, halved, deseeded and sliced

2 tablespoons extra virgin olive oil

1 teaspoon herbes de provence

1 large shallot, chopped

a large handful of flat leaf parsley, chopped

coarse sea salt and freshly ground black pepper

vinaigrette

2 teaspoons cumin seeds

3 tablespoons wine vinegar

1 teaspoon fine sea salt

150 ml extra virgin olive oil

serves 6

carbohydrate 25 g

One day before serving, soak the chickpeas in cold water to cover, and put in the refrigerator. Next day, drain the chickpeas. Transfer to a saucepan and cover with cold water. Add the bay leaf and bring to the boil. When the water boils, lower the heat, cover and simmer until tender, about 2 hours. Check occasionally and add more water if necessary. Add 1 teaspoon coarse sea salt 30 minutes before the end of cooking time.

Meanwhile, put the peppers in a small baking dish, toss with the oil, herbs and 1 teaspoon salt. Roast in a preheated oven at 220°C (425°F) Gas 7 until beginning to char, 20–25 minutes. Remove from the oven. When cool, cut into dice and set aside.

To make the vinaigrette, dry-fry the cumin seeds in a hot frying pan until they begin to pop and you can smell their aroma. Immediately crush them to a powder with a mortar and pestle.

Put the vinegar in a small bowl. Using a fork or a small whisk, stir in the fine sea salt until almost dissolved. You may have to tilt the bowl so the vinegar is deep enough to have something to stir. Add the olive oil, a tablespoon at a time, whisking well between each addition, until emulsified. Mix in the cumin and add pepper to taste.

When the chickpeas are cooked, drain thoroughly and transfer to a serving bowl; a wide, shallow one is best, to ensure the maximum amount of dressing comes into contact with the chickpeas. Add the vinaigrette, red pepper and shallot. Toss well and add salt and pepper to taste. Add the parsley, toss again and serve warm or at room temperature.

There are a wide variety of lentils and among the most flavoursome are the small French Puy lentils, which are a pretty maroon colour. To enhance their flavour, you can add aromatics such as onion, herbs or garlic to the cooking water. Although feta cheese is Greek or Cypriot, rather than Italian, it goes very well in this salad.

lentil and feta salad

200 g Puy lentils,

4 preserved baby artichokes, preferably char-grilled, quartered

1 red onion, thinly sliced

150 g feta cheese, cut into cubes or crumbled into big pieces

a handful of mixed fresh herbs, such as parsley, basil or marjoram, coarsely chopped, or chives, to serve

sea salt

italian dressing

1 tablespoon cider vinegar

3–4 tablespoons extra virgin olive oil

freshly ground black pepper

serves 4

carbohydrate 27 g

Put the lentils in a saucepan and cover with plenty of cold water. Bring to the boil and simmer gently for 25 minutes, or according to the instructions on the packet, until tender, but still firm. Drain well and set aside.

Meanwhile, to make the dressing, put the vinegar and oil in a bowl, season with pepper and beat with a fork or small whisk.

Put the lentils in a salad bowl, then add the dressing and stir to coat.

Add the artichokes, onion and feta cheese, then toss gently. Add salt, if necessary, and pepper to taste, then serve, sprinkled with herbs.

Variations If you prefer, you can replace the feta cheese with bocconcini or mozzarella cheese, torn into long shreds, or shredded roasted chicken. Black olives also make a tasty addition.

The main ingredients in this substantial vegetarian salad are protein-rich lentils and antioxidant tomatoes. Sumac is a popular Middle Eastern spice enjoyed for its sour flavour. Serve this salad as a side dish with grilled fish or meat.

tomato and lentil salad

200 g brown lentils

5 tablespoons extra virgin olive oil

1 onion, halved and thinly sliced

400 g cherry tomatoes, quartered

2 teaspoons sumac, plus extra to serve (optional)*

sea salt and freshly ground black pepper

serves 6

carbohydrate 21 g

Put the lentils in a bowl, cover with plenty of cold water and soak for 2 hours or according to the instructions on the packet. Drain, transfer to a saucepan, add a pinch of salt and cover with boiling water. Return to the boil, reduce the heat and simmer for 15 minutes or until tender, but still firm. Drain well and set aside.

Clean the pan, add 2 tablespoons of the olive oil, heat well, then add the onion. Fry gently for about 8 minutes until softened and translucent. Remove from the heat and add the lentils, tomatoes, sumac, if using, salt, pepper and the remaining oil. Stir gently with a wooden spoon and serve as a side dish, with extra sumac served separately.

Note If you can't find sumac but would like to try this salad, try caraway seeds, which will give this salad a light anise flavour rather than the sour edge provided by the sumac. Add 1 teaspoon caraway seeds when you heat the oil, then proceed with the recipe.

1 large tuna steak, about 250 g, or 2 small cans good-quality tuna, about 160 g each, drained

6 tablespoons olive oil, plus extra for brushing

2 red onions, thinly sliced

2–3 large garlic cloves, crushed

1 tablespoon sherry vinegar or white wine vinegar

500 g cooked or canned green flageolet beans, white cannellini beans, or a mixture of both

4 handfuls of fresh basil leaves and small sprigs

sea salt and freshly ground black pepper

a ridged stove-top grill pan

serves 4–6

carbohydrate 10 g

An Italian classic, this dish is traditionally made with good-quality canned tuna, but you can use fresh tuna, a good source of Omega-3 polyunsaturated fatty acids. White cannellini beans are usual, but green flageolets have a distinctive flavour and pretty colour.

italian tuna and beans

If using fresh tuna, brush with olive oil and put on a preheated ridged stove-top grill pan. Cook for 3 minutes on each side or until barred with brown but pink in the middle (the time depends on the thickness of the fish). Remove from the pan, cool and pull into chunks.

Put the oil, onions, crushed garlic and vinegar in a bowl and beat with a fork. Add the beans and toss gently until well coated.

Add the tuna and basil and season with salt and pepper, then serve.

3 fillets fine-textured fish with red, pink or silver skins, such as snapper, sea bass or bream, about 750 g

freshly squeezed juice of 2 limes

freshly squeezed juice of 2 lemons

2 pink Thai shallots or 1 regular shallot, halved and thinly sliced

3 cm fresh ginger, peeled and sliced into thin matchsticks

200 ml coconut cream

1 green serrano chilli, deseeded and thinly sliced

1 red serrano chilli, deseeded and thinly sliced

6 spring onions, thinly sliced

a small handful of fresh coriander

6 sprigs of Chinese flowering chives (optional)

6 lime wedges, to serve

serves 6

carbohydrate 4 g

This marinated fish salad from the Philippines uses the same technique of 'cooking' the fish in lime juice as the Mexican dish ceviche – the acid in the juice changes the texture of the fish and the flesh becomes opaque. If you can't find Chinese flowering chives (also known as *kuchai* and sold in Chinese markets), use regular chives and a small crushed garlic clove.

filipino marinated fish salad
with chives

Cut the fish crossways into 5-cm pieces and put in a glass or china dish. Pour over the lime and lemon juices and sprinkle with the shallots and ginger. Cover with clingfilm and set aside for 4 hours in the refrigerator.

Drain the juices from the fish and mix the juices with the coconut cream. Arrange the fish in a serving dish, pour over the coconut cream mixture and top with the chillies, spring onions, coriander and Chinese flowering chives, if using. Serve the lime wedges separately.

750 g fresh squid tubes, with tentacles

100 g pink Thai shallots or regular shallots

1 stalk of lemongrass, trimmed and thinly sliced

2 long red chillies, deseeded and thinly sliced

3 kaffir lime leaves, rolled up and thinly sliced

2 cm fresh ginger, peeled, thinly sliced, then cut into thin matchsticks

3 spring onions, sliced diagonally

sea salt

dressing

2 garlic cloves, crushed

2 medium red chillies, finely chopped

freshly squeezed juice of 4 small limes

4 tablespoons Thai fish sauce

to serve

2 tablespoons chopped mint or Thai mint

a handful of Thai basil leaves (page 123)

serves 6

carbohydrate 7 g

Squid is a good source of protein, as well as being low-carb and low-GI, and this spicy Thai squid salad is a delicious summer starter, full of light and interesting flavours. Scoring the inside of the squid will not only tenderize it, but also make it curl attractively when cooked. Try to find Thai mint as it tastes fabulous when chopped, adding a heat that's not to be missed.

thai spicy squid salad

To make the dressing, pound the garlic and chillies with a mortar and pestle, then add the lime juice and fish sauce. Transfer to a serving bowl and chill until needed.

Cut the squid tubes down one edge to make 1 large piece. Score the inside with a diamond pattern and cut each piece diagonally in half.

Prepare a saucepan of boiling salted water and drop the squid into the water in 2 batches. As soon as they curl up, leave for 1 minute more and drain immediately. Make sure to bring the water back to the boil again before dropping in the next batch. Add the squid to the chilled dressing in the serving bowl while still hot.

Add the shallots, lemongrass, chillies, kaffir lime leaves, ginger and spring onions to the bowl and toss gently. Serve sprinkled with the chopped mint and whole Thai basil leaves.

1 cos or iceberg lettuce, quartered and torn apart

about 250 g feta cheese, crumbled into big pieces or cut into cubes

about 200 g Kalamata olives

2 red onions, halved, then sliced into petals

2 mini cucumbers, halved lengthways, then thinly sliced diagonally

4 big ripe red tomatoes, cut into chunks

8 anchovy fillets, or to taste

a few sprigs of oregano, torn

a few sprigs of mint, torn

greek dressing

6 tablespoons extra virgin olive oil

2 tablespoons freshly squeezed lemon juice

sea salt and freshly ground black pepper

serves 4

carbohydrate 14 g

Greek salads are very much a part of the Mediterranean style of eating – crisp cucumber, juicy tomatoes, a few baby herbs, some vinegary olives and salty feta. Greek Kalamata olives are among the world's best – unpitted ones have more flavour, but be careful about the stones. Though anchovies aren't traditional, they are delicious in this salad. Serve it as a communal dish before the main course.

big greek salad

Put the lettuce in a big bowl. Add the cheese, olives, onions, cucumbers and tomatoes.

To make the dressing, put the olive oil, lemon juice, salt and pepper in a jug or bowl and beat with a fork, then pour over the salad. You can also sprinkle them onto the salad separately.

Top with the anchovies, oregano and mint, then serve.

Variation Authentic Greek salads often include green pepper. Halve, deseed and slice horizontally before adding.

warm chicken salad

with harissa dressing

2 punnets ripe cherry tomatoes, or 4 sprays of cherry or plum tomatoes on the vine

olive oil, for roasting

½ garlic clove, crushed

4 freshly cooked chicken breasts

salad leaves

20 large green or black olives, pitted and halved

2 red onions, halved, then cut into thin wedges lengthways

sea salt and freshly ground black pepper

harissa dressing

6 tablespoons extra virgin olive oil

1 tablespoon harissa paste*

1 tablespoon cider or sherry vinegar

a baking sheet

serves 4

carbohydrate 10 g

Everyone loves a chicken salad and chicken breast is perfect for a low-carb diet. Whether the chicken is roasted, poached or char-grilled, the important thing is that the salad should be prepared while the chicken is still warm. Don't just chop a chilled cooked chicken breast. Take a just-cooked breast and pull it into large pieces. It separates along the grain, tastes better and is more tender.

Put the tomatoes on a baking sheet – if using vine tomatoes, put the whole vine on the sheet. Sprinkle with salt and olive oil, plus crushed garlic, and roast in a preheated oven at 200°C (400°F) Gas 6 or higher, until slightly charred and starting to collapse. Let cool, but do not chill.

Mix the dressing ingredients in a salad bowl and beat with a fork.

While still warm, pull the chicken into long chunks. Add to the bowl, then add the salad leaves, olives and onions and toss gently in the dressing.

Put onto salad plates, add the tomatoes and serve.

*Notes Dressings made with smoky, spicy harissa paste are delicious. Brands of harissa vary in heat, so add a little, taste, then add more if you prefer. Alternatively, you might like regular mustard instead.

6 thick sirloin steaks,
about 1.5 kg total

oil, for brushing

sea salt and freshly ground
black pepper

chimichurri

1 small shallot, chopped

3 garlic cloves, crushed

6 sprigs of oregano

a large bunch of purple basil

1 stalk of fresh green
peppercorns, or 1 tablespoon
green peppercorns preserved
in brine

150 ml olive oil

1 tablespoon red wine vinegar

1 red chilli, deseeded
and finely chopped

to serve

a large bunch of very
fresh watercress, trimmed

sprigs of purple basil

a ridged stove-top grill pan

serves 6

carbohydrate 1 g

This Argentinian pesto-like salsa is usually made with parsley and is served in individual small bowls with thick, rare, char-grilled steaks. The watercress that accompanies it is rich in antioxidants and minerals and adds a fresh peppery taste to the meal. In this recipe, purple or 'opal' basil adds a minty, clove-like quality.

watercress and chimichurri
with char-grilled steak

To make the chimichurri, pound the shallot and garlic to a coarse paste using a mortar and pestle*.

Pull the leaves off the sprigs of oregano and basil and pound into the paste. Remove the peppercorns from the stalk and pound them into the paste. Start adding the oil a little at a time, then pound in the vinegar and chilli, keeping the mixture chunky.

Brush the steaks with oil and season well. Heat a ridged stove-top grill pan and, when it starts to smoke, add the steaks and cook for about 1½–2 minutes on each side. Remove them and let rest in a warm place for 5 minutes. Slice thickly and serve with the chimichurri, watercress and basil.

Note It is traditional to use a mortar and pestle to make the chimichurri. However, use a blender to save time if you prefer, pulsing to keep the paste as coarse as possible.

soups

Classic in its simplicity, miso soup warms and entices at the beginning of a Japanese meal. *Shichimi togarashi* (Japanese seven-spice blend), kombu and wakame are all widely available in larger supermarkets, Asian and wholefood stores. Serve this simple and delicious soup as the Japanese do, in beautiful lacquer bowls.

miso and wakame soup
with japanese seven-spice

2 tablespoons wakame (dried seaweed)

3 tablespoons miso paste

125 g firm tofu, cut into 1-cm cubes

1 spring onion, trimmed and finely chopped

Japanese seven-spice (shichimi togarashi) or ground sansho pepper, to serve (optional)

dashi*

1 piece kombu (dried kelp), 5 cm square

15 g dried bonito flakes, about 6 tablespoons

serves 4

carbohydrate 4 g

To make the dashi, put the kombu in a large saucepan and add 550 ml water. Bring to the boil and immediately remove the kombu (don't let it boil or it will become bitter).

Add the bonito flakes to the boiling water, simmer gently for 2–3 minutes, then remove from the heat. Let stand for a few minutes until the bonito settles to the bottom of the pan. Strain through a sieve lined with muslin and reserve the liquid. Alternatively, add 1–2 teaspoons instant dashi powder to the boiling water and stir to dissolve.

Meanwhile, soak the wakame in a large bowl of water for 10–15 minutes until fully opened. Drain and cut into small pieces.

Put the miso paste in a cup or bowl and mix with a few spoonfuls of dashi. Return the dashi to a low heat and add the diluted miso paste. Add the wakame and tofu to the pan and turn up the heat. Just before it reaches boiling point, add the spring onion and immediately remove from the heat. Do not boil.

Serve hot in large soup bowls sprinkled with a little Japanese seven-spice, if using.

*Note Instant dashi powder is widely available in larger supermarkets and Japanese stores. Labelled 'dashi-no-moto', it is freeze-dried and very convenient. Use 1–2 teaspoons for this recipe.

One of the great classics of the soup world is pea and ham. It used to be a staple made after the Christmas holidays, when only the bone and a few shreds of meat were left from the ham. These were cooked with dried green peas and water to form a lovely, comforting, warming winter soup. This is an all-year-round version using fresh or frozen peas.

fresh pea soup
with mint and crispy bacon

1 tablespoon olive oil

4–8 slices very thinly cut smoked streaky bacon or smoked pancetta

500 g shelled green peas, fresh or frozen

1 litre boiling ham stock, chicken stock or water

sea salt and freshly ground black pepper

to serve (optional)

4 tablespoons single cream

sprigs of mint

serves 4

carbohydrate 15 g

Heat the olive oil in a frying pan, add the bacon and sauté until crisp. Remove and drain on crumpled kitchen paper, or drape over a wooden spoon so they curl.

To cook the peas, microwave on HIGH for 3–4 minutes, or follow the packet instructions. Alternatively, simmer in boiling water with a pinch of salt for 2–3 minutes or until tender. Drain.

Put the peas in a blender with 1–2 ladles of stock or water. Work to a purée, adding extra stock if necessary. Add the remaining stock and blend again. Taste and adjust the seasoning. Reheat, thinning with a little boiling water if necessary, then ladle into heated soup bowls and serve, topped with the crisp bacon, a swirl of cream and mint sprigs, if using.

Variation Cook the peas, drain and let cool, then put in the blender with 8 ice cubes and enough water to make the blades run. Blend to a purée, then thin with iced water to the consistency you like. Add salt and pepper to taste and serve topped with sliced spring onions.

A typical way to thicken and enrich a broth in many parts of Italy is to add protein-rich beaten eggs rather than flour or cornflour. This is one of the best Italian soups because of the freshness of the greens. Although spinach is traditional (and a good source of vitamins and minerals), try other varieties of greens – beetroot tops, for example, or even courgette leaves and tendrils.

spinach broth
with egg and cheese

700 g fresh spinach

50 g butter

4 eggs

5 tablespoons freshly grated Parmesan cheese

¼ teaspoon freshly grated nutmeg

about 1.75 litres chicken stock

sea salt and freshly ground black pepper

serves 6

carbohydrate 2 g

Remove all the stalks from the spinach, then wash the leaves thoroughly – do not shake dry. Cook the leaves in a large saucepan with the water still clinging. When the leaves have wilted, drain well, then chop finely.

Heat the butter in a medium saucepan, then add the spinach, tossing well to coat with the butter. Remove from the heat and let cool for 5 minutes.

Put the eggs, Parmesan, nutmeg, salt and pepper in a bowl and beat well. Mix into the spinach. Put the stock in a large saucepan and bring almost to the boil. When almost boiling, whisk in the spinach and egg mixture as quickly as you can to avoid curdling. Reheat gently without boiling for a couple of minutes and serve immediately.

pumpkin and coconut soup

groundnut oil, for roasting and greasing

1 kg pumpkin, cut into wedges, but unpeeled

250 ml canned thick coconut milk

1 litre hot chicken stock

sea salt and freshly ground black pepper

to serve (optional)

4 red bird's eye chillies, thinly sliced

fresh coconut, shaved with a vegetable peeler, about 2–4 tablespoons

freshly grated nutmeg

a baking sheet

serves 4

carbohydrate 6 g

Pumpkin soup is a great favourite in Australia and New Zealand, where pumpkin is such a popular vegetable that it is one of the three served with the Sunday roast. This soup can be made with boiled or roasted pumpkin. The coconut milk makes it sweet and creamy, while the chilli enhances the flavour. If you can't find a dense-fleshed pumpkin with grey or green skin, use butternut squash.

Brush the baking sheet with oil, add the pumpkin wedges and brush them with oil too. Cook in a preheated oven at 200°C (400°F) Gas 6 until browned outside and soft and fluffy inside, about 30 minutes, according to the size of the chunks. Scrape the flesh out of the skins and discard the skins. Alternatively, boil peeled pumpkin in lightly salted water until tender, then drain.

Put the pumpkin in a blender, add salt, the coconut milk and a ladle of hot stock. Purée until smooth and creamy, in batches if necessary, adding more stock as required.

Transfer to a clean saucepan, season to taste with salt and pepper and reheat to just below boiling point. Ladle into heated soup bowls, top with the chillies, coconut shavings and a little nutmeg, if using, then serve.

This is a soup to make if you grow your own tomatoes, have access to a farmer who sells them at the farm gate, or there's a good farmers' market nearby. The tomatoes must be very ripe and full of flavour. Basil, the quintessential herb to accompany tomatoes, here makes a luscious pesto. Don't boil the soup or it will lose its fresh taste.

tomato soup with pesto

1 kg very ripe red tomatoes

500 ml chicken stock, or to taste

grated zest and freshly squeezed juice of 1 unwaxed lemon

4 tablespoons pesto*

scissor-snipped chives or torn basil (optional)

sea salt and freshly ground black pepper

serves 4

carbohydrate 9 g

To skin the tomatoes, cut a cross in the base of each and dunk into a saucepan of boiling water. Remove after 10 seconds and put in a strainer set over a large saucepan. Slip off and discard the skins and cut the tomatoes in half crossways. Using a teaspoon, deseed into the strainer, then press the pulp and juice through the strainer and add to the blender. Discard the seeds. Chop the tomato halves and add to the blender. Alternatively, put through a mouli food mill.

Purée the tomatoes, in batches, if necessary, adding a little of the stock to help the process. Add the remaining stock, season to taste with salt and pepper and transfer to the saucepan. Heat well without boiling. Serve in heated soup plates topped with a spoonful of lemon juice, pesto, chives, if using, lemon zest and pepper.

*Note To make your own pesto, put 4 tablespoons pine nuts in a dry frying pan and fry gently and quickly until golden (about 30 seconds). They burn easily, so don't leave them. Remove to a plate and let cool. Transfer to a food processor or blender, add 4 crushed garlic cloves, 1 teaspoon sea salt and the leaves from a very large bunch of basil. Purée to a paste, in pulses if necessary. Add 25 g freshly grated Parmesan cheese and blend again. Add 125 ml extra virgin olive oil and blend until smooth. Add extra oil if you want a looser texture.

2 tablespoons extra
virgin olive oil

1 red pepper, halved,
deseeded and sliced

1 onion, halved and sliced

3 garlic cloves, crushed

1 green chilli, deseeded
and chopped

¼ teaspoon oak-smoked hot
Spanish pimentón (paprika)

a sprig of thyme

225 g canned chopped
peeled tomatoes

1.5 litres fresh fish stock

250 g monkfish fillet,
cut into bite-sized pieces

500 g hake or cod steaks

250 g prawn tails, shells on

250 ml dry white wine

500 g fresh mussels*

a handful of fresh flat leaf
parsley, chopped

serves 4–6

carbohydrate 8 g

You can make this nutritious soup with whatever fish are plentiful on the day, and if you use good-quality fresh fish stock, it's very quick to make. The bones and prawn shells add flavour, as well as making it a bit messy, but this is fishermen's fare, so roll up your sleeves and enjoy. Serve as a starter or main course.

basque fish soup

Heat the oil in a stockpot. Add the pepper and onion and cook until browned, about 5 minutes. Stir in the garlic, chilli, paprika, thyme and tomatoes and cook for 5 minutes more.

Add the fish stock, monkfish, hake and prawns. Bring to the boil, then skim off the foam. Simmer gently until the fish is cooked through, about 10–15 minutes.

Pour the wine into a large saucepan with a lid and bring to the boil for 1 minute, then remove from the heat. Add the prepared mussels to the wine, cover and steam over high heat just until opened, 2–3 minutes. Remove the mussels from their shells, discarding any that do not open.

Add the mussels and cooking liquid to the soup and stir well. Sprinkle with parsley and serve immediately.

*Note To prepare mussels, start 15 minutes before you are ready to use. Rinse them in cold water and tap any open ones against the work surface. If they don't close, discard them. Scrub the others with a stiff brush and scrape off any barnacles. Pull off and discard the wiry beards.

chicken soup with vegetables

a handful of mini asparagus tips, halved crossways

a large handful of sugar snap peas, cut into 2–3 pieces each

1 punnet cherry tomatoes, quartered and deseeded

sea salt and freshly ground black pepper

south-east asian chicken stock

1 small organic chicken

2 whole star anise

2 cinnamon sticks

a handful of kaffir lime leaves

2 stalks of lemongrass, halved lengthways and bruised

7 cm fresh ginger, peeled and sliced

4 garlic cloves, lightly crushed but whole

1 red chilli, halved lengthways

1 tablespoon black peppercorns, bruised

to serve

1 chilli, red or green, sliced

fresh herbs, such as coriander, Chinese chives, parsley or regular chives

serves 4

carbohydrate 4 g

The basis of this soup is the simplest, best and tastiest chicken stock in the world – an Asian stock full of wonderful flavours of the Orient. The better the chicken, the better the stock, so invest in the best chicken you can find – organic, free-range and all those desirable things. Don't overcook the vegetables – they need to retain their crispness and flavour.

Put all the chicken stock ingredients in a large saucepan, add water to cover the chicken by 3 cm, bring to the boil, reduce the heat and simmer for at least 1 hour.

Remove the chicken, whole, from the pan and reserve. Scoop out the solids from the stock, reserving the ginger. Put the ginger on a plate and cut into tiny slivers.

Strain the stock into a saucepan, ladling at first, then pouring through muslin. It should be clear but slightly fatty on top. Blot off any excess fat, if you prefer.

Taste the stock and reduce if necessary. Season to taste. Pull shreds of chicken off the bird and cut into bite-sized pieces if necessary. Put in a bowl and cover.

Return the stock to the boil, add the ginger slivers and thick parts of the asparagus and blanch for 30 seconds. Add the asparagus tips and blanch for 3 seconds more. Add the peas, tomatoes and chicken and blanch for 30 seconds. You are heating them and keeping the peas and tomatoes fresh, rather than cooking them to a mush. Ladle into large soup bowls and top with sliced chilli and the herb of your choice.

1.25 litres boiling chicken stock, preferably homemade

350 g boneless, skinless chicken breasts, thinly sliced

2 garlic cloves, chopped

2 stalks of lemongrass, halved lengthways

3 tablespoons Thai fish sauce, or light soy sauce

3 cm fresh ginger, peeled and grated

3 cm fresh galangal, peeled and sliced (optional)

8 small spring onions, quartered

250 ml canned coconut milk

4 fresh kaffir lime leaves, crushed (optional)

2 fresh green bird's eye chillies, crushed

a large handful of fresh coriander leaves, torn

250 g uncooked tiger prawns, tails only, shelled or unshelled

freshly squeezed juice of 2 limes

serves 4

carbohydrate 3 g

This must be one of the world's best-loved soups as it's utterly superb. Fresh lemongrass, galangal, kaffir lime leaves and fiery bird's eye chillies will require a visit to a Thai or Chinese grocer or supermarket. Powdered substitutes will not do.

spicy thai chicken soup

Put the chicken stock in a large saucepan and bring to the boil. Add the chicken, garlic, lemongrass, fish sauce, ginger, galangal, if using, spring onions and coconut milk.

Return to the boil, part-cover, then reduce the heat to a high simmer and cook for 5 minutes. Add the kaffir lime leaves, if using, the chillies, half the coriander leaves and the prawns.

Simmer gently for 5 minutes, or until the chicken is cooked through and the prawn flesh is opaque – do not overcook or the prawns will be tough. Add the lime juice and serve in large soup bowls, topped with the remaining coriander.

Note Remove the chillies before eating the soup: they are fiery, but leaving them whole and merely crushing them releases a gentle, not violent heat.

750 g trimmed braising beef, cut into small chunks

7 white peppercorns

3 cm fresh galangal, peeled and sliced, or fresh ginger

1 teaspoon freshly grated nutmeg

¼ teaspoon ground turmeric

325 ml coconut milk

sea salt

spice paste

2–3 tablespoons groundnut oil

1 teaspoon ground coriander

7 white peppercorns

4 red bird's eye chillies

2 teaspoons brown sugar

1 garlic clove, chopped

5 fresh Thai basil leaves (page 123)

a large handful of fresh coriander, about 25 g, coarsely chopped

8 pink Thai shallots or 1 regular shallot

a few cardamom seeds (not pods)

2 cm fresh ginger, peeled and chopped

½ teaspoon shrimp paste (blachan or belacan)*, toasted in a dry frying pan or the oven

serves 4–6

carbohydrate 7 g

This low-carb Indonesian soup is a fascinating mixture of spices and flavours. Slices of simmered beef are immersed in a creamy broth enlivened by a hot, spicy paste. It's warming and filling and makes a great main course or starter.

indonesian beef and coconut soup

Put all the spice paste ingredients into a blender or a food processor and grind to a thick paste, adding a dash of water to keep the blades turning if necessary. Set aside.

Put the beef, peppercorns, galangal, nutmeg, turmeric and salt into a saucepan, add 1.5 litres water and bring to the boil, skimming off the foam as it rises to the surface. Stir, reduce the heat and simmer uncovered for about 1½ hours, until the meat is mostly tender and the stock is well reduced.

Strain the beef, discarding the galangal slices and peppercorns, but reserving the beef and stock. Return the stock to the pan, then stir in the spice paste. Bring to the boil, reduce the heat, add the beef and simmer for 5 minutes, stirring regularly.

Finally, add the coconut milk and simmer gently for a few minutes, then serve.

*Note Sold in Asian food stores, dried shrimp paste is extremely pungent and gives a distinctive taste to South-east Asian food. It should always be toasted before using. Simply wrap a piece in foil and toast it in a hot oven until it darkens – for a few minutes each side. Open the kitchen windows while you do this as it leaves a pervasive scent. If you can't find dried shrimp paste, use 1 teaspoon anchovy paste mixed with 1 teaspoon Thai fish sauce.

Containing virtually no carbohydrates, mushrooms are high in fibre and protein. The flavour of dried porcini mushrooms is highly concentrated and just a few will add a strong flavour to a soup made with regular cultivated mushrooms. For a deeper colour as well as flavour, use large Portobello mushrooms.

cream of mushroom soup

25 g dried porcini mushrooms

4 tablespoons olive oil

6 large portobello mushrooms, wiped, trimmed and sliced

1 onion, halved and thinly sliced

3 garlic cloves, crushed

a pinch of freshly grated nutmeg

a large bunch of parsley, finely chopped in a food processor

1¼ litres boiling chicken or vegetable stock

sea salt and freshly ground black pepper

to serve

4–6 tablespoons coarsely chopped fresh parsley (optional)

4–6 tablespoons crème fraîche

serves 4–6

carbohydrate 8 g

Put the dried porcini in a bowl, add 250 ml boiling water and let soak for at least 15 minutes. Heat the oil in a frying pan, add the fresh mushrooms and sauté until coloured but still firm. Reserve a few slices for serving.

Add the onion to the frying pan and sauté until softened, then add the garlic, nutmeg and parsley. Rinse any grit out of the porcini and strain their soaking liquid several times through muslin or a tea strainer. Add the liquid and the porcini to the pan. Bring to the boil, then transfer to a food processor. Add 2 ladles of the boiling stock, then pulse until creamy but still chunky.

Put the remaining stock in a saucepan, then add the mushroom mixture, bring to the boil and simmer for 20 minutes. Add salt and pepper to taste, then serve topped with a few reserved mushrooms, parsley, if using, and a spoonful of crème fraîche.

Note If you use a blender to make the soup, the purée will be very smooth. If you use a food processor, it will be less smooth, and if you use the pulse button, you can make the mixture quite chunky.

tuscan bean soup with rosemary

This simple soup is found in various guises all over central and northern Italy. To give it a sophisticated touch, fry sliced garlic, rosemary and chilli in really good olive oil, just enough to release their aroma, then spoon this over the soup just before serving. Like many other rugged soups, it is often served as a main course.

250 g dried white or brown beans (such as haricot, borlotti or cannellini)

a pinch of bicarbonate of soda

cold water, or chicken or vegetable stock

a handful of fresh sage leaves, plus 2 tablespoons chopped fresh sage

4 garlic cloves

300 ml olive oil

2 tablespoons chopped fresh rosemary

a large pinch of dried chilli flakes

sea salt and freshly ground black pepper

coarsely chopped fresh flat leaf parsley, to serve

serves 6

carbohydrate 22 g

Put the beans in a bowl, cover with cold water, add a pinch of bicarbonate of soda, soak overnight, then drain just before you're ready to use them.

Put the drained beans in a flameproof casserole. Cover with cold water or chicken or vegetable stock to a depth of 5 cm above the beans, and push in the handful of sage. Bring to the boil, cover tightly with a lid and transfer to a preheated oven at 160°C (325°F) Gas 3 for about 1 hour or until tender. (The time depends on the freshness of the beans – test after 40 minutes.) Keep them in their cooking liquid.

Meanwhile, finely chop 2 of the garlic cloves, and thinly slice the remainder. Put half the beans, the cooked sage (minus any stalks), and all the liquid in a blender or food processor and blend until smooth. Pour back into the remaining beans in the casserole. If the soup is thicker than you like, add extra water or stock to thin it down.

Heat half the olive oil in a frying pan and add the chopped garlic. Fry gently until soft and golden, then add the chopped sage and cook for 30 seconds. Stir this into the soup and reheat until boiling. Simmer gently for 10 minutes. Add salt and pepper to taste.

Pour into a heated tureen or soup bowls. Heat the remaining olive oil in a small frying pan, add the sliced garlic and fry carefully until golden (don't let it go too dark or it will be bitter). Stir in the rosemary and chilli flakes. Dip the base of the frying pan in cold water to stop the garlic cooking. Spoon the garlic and oil over the soup, then serve sprinkled with parsley.

50 g butter

50 g pancetta

150 g fresh wild mushrooms or dark portobello mushrooms, plus 25 g dried porcini mushrooms, soaked in warm water for 20 minutes to soften, then drained

2 shallots, finely chopped

2 garlic cloves, coarsely chopped

freshly squeezed juice of 1 lemon

400 g canned chickpeas, drained

1.5 litres chicken or vegetable stock

150 ml double cream

3 tablespoons freshly chopped flat leaf parsley

sea salt and freshly ground black pepper

serves 6

carbohydrate 13 g

The combination of creamy chickpeas, smoky bacon and earthy mushrooms in this tasty soup is unusual and captivating. Wild mushrooms have a strong, almost meaty taste; try to get a good selection of different varieties. The dried porcini will add extra depth of flavour. This is a comforting soup, rich and creamy, with the parsley, stirred in at the end, giving it a dash of colour.

cream of chickpea soup
with wild mushrooms

Put the butter in a large saucepan, melt gently, then add the pancetta and fry slowly until golden.

Put the mushrooms, shallots and garlic in a food processor and chop finely, using the pulse button. Add the mushroom mixture to the pancetta and cook, stirring over medium to high heat, for about 15 minutes, until all the juices have evaporated and the mixture becomes a thick paste. Stir in the lemon juice and chickpeas. Whisk in the stock and bring to the boil. Cover and simmer for 25 minutes.

Transfer the soup, in batches if necessary, to a blender or food processor and blend until smooth. Return the soup to the rinsed-out pan and stir in the cream. Add salt and pepper to taste, then stir in the parsley and reheat without boiling, or the soup may curdle.

fish and seafood

Moules marinière is the best-known mussel dish, but this simple recipe for steamed mussels means that you can put it in the oven, put the timer on for 10 minutes and not worry about it in the meantime. Mussels are a good source of Omega-3 fatty acids and parsley is rich in vitamin C. To serve as a main course for two people, just halve the ingredients and make two parcels.

steamed mussels in a parcel

1 kg fresh mussels
50 g butter
150 ml dry vermouth
2 garlic cloves, crushed
a bunch of flat leaf parsley, coarsely chopped, to serve

4 pieces of foil, about 60 x 30 cm
a baking sheet

serves 4

carbohydrate 5 g

Scrub the mussels well, knock off any barnacles and pull off the beards. Discard any broken mussels and any that won't close when they are tapped on the work surface. Drain in a colander.

Fold each piece of foil in half lengthways and divide the butter, vermouth, garlic and mussels among them. Bring the corners of each piece together to close each parcel, leaving a little space in each one so the mussels will have room to open. Pinch the edges of the parcels together to seal.

Put the parcels on a baking sheet, transfer to a preheated oven and cook at 200°C (400°F) Gas 6 for 10–12 minutes until all the mussels have opened – check by opening one of the parcels. Serve the parcels on warmed plates, with a bowl of chopped parsley to sprinkle over the mussels.

Mediterranean live clams usually go straight into the cooking pot, with oil and garlic. Herbs and a splash of wine are also sometimes added, as here. However, because Spanish cured hams are so exceptional, adding even a little will season and enliven many savoury dishes, such as this.

spanish clams with ham

2 tablespoons
extra virgin olive oil

500 g live clams in the shell,
or frozen raw clams

50 g serrano or Parma ham, cut
into thin strips

1 small green chilli,
deseeded and chopped

2 garlic cloves, sliced

4 tablespoons
white wine or cider

2 tablespoons chopped spring
onion tops, chives or parsley

serves 4

carbohydrate 3 g

Put the olive oil, clams, ham, chilli and garlic in a flameproof casserole and stir over high heat. When the ham is cooked and the clams begin to open, add the wine, cover the pan and tilt it several times to mix the ingredients. Cook on high for a further 2–3 minutes or until all the clams have opened and are cooked.

Sprinkle with chopped spring onion tops. Cover again for 1 minute, then ladle into shallow soup bowls.

char-grilled spiced prawns

1 kg large, uncooked tiger prawns, shells on

spice mix

2 tablespoons mild or hot paprika

1 teaspoon dried red chillies, crushed

4 tablespoons garam masala*

2 teaspoons ground turmeric

1 teaspoon coriander seeds, crushed

1 tablespoon sea salt flakes

5 cm fresh ginger, grated

4 garlic cloves, crushed

125 g ghee or clarified butter, melted

2 limes

8 wooden or bamboo skewers, soaked in water for 30 minutes

serves 4

carbohydrate 10 g

All shellfish is low-carb and for these spicy kebabs use whatever large prawns are available: tiger prawns, king prawns, even baby lobsters or crayfish. In India, the garam masala in the spice mix is different from cook to cook, and area to area, but often includes black pepper, black cumin, cinnamon, cloves, mace, cardamom, bay and red chillies. It is always best freshly ground.

Slash the curved backs of the prawns, then remove and discard any black threads. Pat the prawns dry with kitchen paper.

To make the spice mix, grind the paprika, dried chillies, garam masala, turmeric, coriander and salt with a mortar and pestle or electric spice grinder. Add the ginger and garlic, then grind to a rough powdery paste. Add the ghee and juice of 1 of the limes. Stir well. Rub the mixture into the prawns, pushing it under the shells so it penetrates the flesh.

Thread 2 prawns onto each skewer, then grill or barbecue over low heat until aromatic: the flesh should be white and firm and the shells pink. Serve with the remaining lime, cut into wedges.

*Note To make your own garam masala, mix 2 tablespoons each of crushed cinnamon, cumin seeds and coriander seeds in a small frying pan. Add 1 tablespoon each of the seeds from green cardamom pods, peppercorns, cloves and ground mace. Dry-toast to release the aromas, then cool, grind in a spice grinder and either use immediately or store in a jar with a tight lid.

20 large uncooked prawns, shells on

1 tablespoon extra virgin olive oil

3 tablespoons sea salt

tomato, avocado and olive salad

4–6 large ripe tomatoes, sliced

1 large ripe avocado, halved, stoned and sliced

50 g pitted black olives

a handful of fresh mint leaves

4 tablespoons extra virgin olive oil

1 tablespoon vincotto or reduced balsamic vinegar*

shavings of fresh Parmesan cheese

sea salt and freshly ground black pepper

to serve

lemon wedges

salad leaves

serves 4

carbohydrate 7 g

Coating the prawns with sea salt protects the flesh during cooking so that when you shell them, the meat inside is sweet and moist. The avocado in the accompanying salad is rich in monounsaturated fat and vitamin E, while the tomatoes contain antioxidants and vitamins. Try to buy good-quality, firm black olives.

salt-crusted prawns
with tomato, avocado and olive salad

To prepare the salad, put the tomatoes and avocado on a plate with the olives and mint. Put the olive oil and vincotto in a jug and stir well, then sprinkle over the salad. Add the Parmesan and salt and pepper to taste.

Using kitchen scissors, cut down the back of each prawn to reveal the intestinal vein. Pull it out and discard. Wash the prawns under cold running water, pat dry with kitchen paper and put in a bowl. Add 1 tablespoon of the olive oil and toss well. Put the salt on a plate then use it to coat the prawns.

Heat the remaining olive oil in a non-stick frying pan. Add the prawns and cook for 3–5 minutes until the prawns turn pink. Alternatively, heat a barbecue to hot and cook for 2–3 minutes on each side until cooked through. Let cool slightly and serve with lemon wedges and salad leaves.

*Note To reduce balsamic vinegar, put 300 ml in a saucepan and boil gently until it has reduced by about two-thirds and has reached the consistency of thick syrup. Let cool, then store in a clean jar or bottle.

2 garlic cloves, chopped

3 cm fresh ginger, peeled
and chopped

2 tablespoons sunflower
or groundnut oil

4 small tomatoes,
skinned and chopped

2 teaspoons white vinegar
(wine or malt)

500 g uncooked shelled
tiger prawns

sea salt

freshly shaved coconut, to serve

masala paste

1 small onion, quartered

grated flesh of ½ coconut,
fresh or frozen

2 black peppercorns

2 red chillies, deseeded

¼ teaspoon ground turmeric

2 teaspoons ground coriander

½ teaspoon black
mustard seeds

tarka spice-fry

1 tablespoon sunflower
or groundnut oil

a few curry leaves (optional)*

a few red chillies, deseeded
and sliced

serves 4

carbohydrate 6 g

Packed with flavour and easy to make, this dish can be put together in no time. Fresh coconut is high in fibre and a good source of minerals. Choose a whole coconut that contains water – shake it to tell – and that has an intact, firm shell, free of mould.

spiced coconut prawns

Put all the masala paste ingredients in a blender and work into a thick paste, adding a dash of water if necessary to let the blades run. Remove and set aside.

Put the garlic and ginger in the clean blender and grind to a paste. Alternatively, use a mortar and pestle.

Heat the 2 tablespoons oil in a wok or non-stick frying pan. Add the garlic and ginger paste and fry for a few seconds. Add the masala paste and stir-fry until the paste leaves the sides of the pan, 8–10 minutes. Add the chopped tomatoes, vinegar, salt and 250 ml water. Bring to the boil, add the prawns, reduce the heat and cook for 2–3 minutes, until the prawns turn pink. Transfer to a serving bowl.

To prepare the tarka spice-fry, heat the oil in a small pan, add the curry leaves, if using, and red chillies and fry for about 45 seconds or so.

Pour the tempered tarka over the prawns, top with shaved coconut and serve.

*Note Curry leaves are always best fresh, and are often available in Indian or South-east Asian markets. Fresh ones may be frozen. If absolutely necessary, dried ones may be used instead. Please note that curry leaves are not related to the grey curry plant grown in some herb gardens.

green thai fish curry

1 tablespoon groundnut oil

400 ml canned coconut milk

750 g thick white fish fillets, such as monkfish, cod or other firm fish

spice paste

1 onion, sliced

3 garlic cloves, chopped

6 small hot fresh green chillies, deseeded and sliced

5 cm fresh root ginger, peeled and sliced

1 teaspoon ground white pepper

1 teaspoon ground coriander

½ teaspoon ground turmeric

½ teaspoon ground cumin

1 teaspoon shrimp paste (blachan or belacan; page 102), toasted in a dry frying pan or an oven

1 tablespoon Thai fish sauce

1 stalk of lemongrass, trimmed and thinly sliced

to serve

sprigs of fresh Thai basil* (optional)

2 limes, halved

serves 4

carbohydrate 5 g

Thai curries are easy to make, quick to cook and totally delicious. The secret is in the mixture of spices and the freshness of the pastes. You can make the paste in a food processor using ground spices or, if you prefer using whole ones, break them down in a coffee grinder kept solely for that purpose. Store unused paste in the refrigerator.

Put all the spice paste ingredients in a food processor and process until a smooth. Alternatively, use a mortar and pestle. Set aside.

Heat the groundnut oil in a wok, add the spice paste and stir-fry for a few seconds to release the aromas. Add the thick portion from the top of the coconut milk, stir well and boil to thicken slightly.

Add the fish and, using a fish slice or spatula, turn the pieces over until they are well coated in the sauce. Reheat to simmering point and cook until they just start to become opaque, about 2 minutes.

Add the remaining coconut milk and continue cooking until the fish is cooked through. Serve topped with Thai basil sprigs, if using, plus the halved limes.

Note Thai basil is quite different from ordinary basil. It is sold in Asian food markets – if you can't find it, just leave it out.

8 red bream or snapper fillets,
about 750 g

oil, for deep-frying

3 red chillies, deseeded and
thinly sliced

2 stalks of lemongrass,
trimmed and thinly sliced

8 pink Thai shallots or 2 regular
shallots, thinly sliced

5 cm fresh ginger, peeled,
thinly sliced and cut into
matchstick strips

6 kaffir lime leaves, rolled
and thinly sliced

12–18 Vietnamese coriander*

6 limes, cut into wedges, to serve

marinade

2 garlic cloves, finely chopped

2 stalks of lemongrass,
trimmed and thinly sliced

1 teaspoon coriander seeds

1 teaspoon Sichuan pepper

1 teaspoon finely ground
star anise

1 teaspoon ground galangal
(Laos powder)

½ teaspoon sea salt

½ teaspoon freshly ground
black pepper

serves 4

carbohydrate 3 g

Fish is a great low-carb food and high in protein. In this simple Thai dish, fillets are marinated in a spicy paste, then briefly deep-fried and served with deep-fried vegetables and herbs. Lemongrass and kaffir lime leaves are classic Thai ingredients, and if you can find pink Thai shallots so much the better.

fried bream thai-style

Cut each fillet in half and slash each piece twice on the skin side.

Put the marinade ingredients in a mortar and pestle and grind to a fine paste. Rub the paste into the slashes and into the flesh side of the fish pieces, then let marinate for 30 minutes.

Meanwhile, fill a wok about one-third full with oil, heat to about 190°C (375°F), or until a piece of noodle will puff up immediately. Add the chillies, lemongrass, shallots, ginger and lime leaves and deep-fry until crispy – work in batches if necessary to ensure a crisp result. Remove from the wok and drain on kitchen paper. Deep-fry the Vietnamese coriander in the same way – the leaves are fragile when crisp. Remove from the wok and drain on kitchen paper. Pour the oil into a heatproof container and let cool.

To cook the fish, wipe any excess marinade off the skin side. Put about 100 ml of the oil back in the wok and heat gently. Working in batches, fry the fish, flesh side down, over medium heat, for 1 minute, then turn the pieces over and fry for 1 minute more. As each piece is cooked, remove from the wok and pile onto plates. Serve topped with the crispy lemongrass mixture, deep-fried Vietnamese coriander and lime wedges.

Note Vietnamese coriander, or laksa leaf, has long, pointed leaves with an aubergine-coloured horseshoe shape in the centre. It is sold in Asian stores – if you can't find it, just leave it out.

Treat yourself to a taste of the Mediterranean with these barbecued, foil-wrapped fish. They are served with olive oil flavoured with garlic, capers, lemon juice and anchovies which makes for an intensely flavoured dish. The aroma when you open the foil parcel is superb.

sea bass parcels

4 medium whole red mullet, sea bass or snapper, about 300g each, or 4 fillets, 150 g each

freshly squeezed juice of 1 lemon

125 ml extra virgin olive oil

8 canned anchovy fillets, chopped

2 garlic cloves, chopped

4 tablespoons tiny pickled capers, drained

a small handful of fresh flat leaf parsley, chopped

sea salt and freshly ground black pepper

4 pieces foil, 25 cm wide, brushed with oil

serves 4

carbohydrate 1 g

Make 2 diagonal slashes in both sides of each fish and rub in salt and pepper. Set each fish on a piece of foil. Sprinkle with half the lemon juice. Take the edges of foil parallel to the fish and pinch and roll them together in a tight seal. Loosely pleat or fold the foil lengthways, then pinch and roll the narrow ends until tightly closed.

Cook in a preheated oven at 180°C (350°F) Gas 4 for 10–15 minutes for fillets, or 20–25 minutes for whole fish, or until the flesh is white and firm (open one to test). Alternatively, cook over a medium barbecue for about 8–12 minutes for whole fish or 6–8 minutes for fillets.

Meanwhile, using a blender or mortar and pestle, blend the oil with the anchovy fillets, garlic and remaining lemon juice to form a purée. Pour in a bowl, then stir in the capers and parsley. Add extra lemon juice to taste.

Put the fish parcels on 4 heated plates. Open each one just enough to drizzle with the sauce, then reseal the parcels and serve.

4 tuna loin steaks,
cut 2.5 cm thick

olive oil, for sprinkling

marinade

4 garlic cloves

3 tablespoons Dijon mustard

2 tablespoons grappa
or brandy

sea salt and freshly ground
black pepper

peperonata

6 tablespoons olive oil

1 kg fresh ripe tomatoes,
skinned, deseeded and
chopped, or 800 g canned
chopped tomatoes

½ teaspoon dried chilli flakes

2 medium onions, thinly sliced

3 garlic cloves, chopped

3 large red peppers, halved,
deseeded and cut into
thin strips

sea salt and freshly ground
black pepper

serves 4

carbohydrate 22 g

Tuna is a very full-bodied meat and is rich in Omega-3 fatty acids. Marinating the slices in mustard and grappa gives them a piquant crust – which goes well with the peppers. Overcooking tuna can make it very dry, so watch it like a hawk – it's better to have it slightly undercooked.

grilled tuna steaks
with peperonata

To make the marinade, crush the garlic, put in a bowl and beat in the mustard and grappa. Season with salt and pepper and use to spread over the cut sides of the tuna. Arrange in a non-metal dish, cover and let marinate in a cool place for about 1 hour.

To make the peperonata, heat 3 tablespoons of the oil in a saucepan, then add the tomatoes and chilli flakes. Cook over medium heat for about 10 minutes until the tomatoes have disintegrated.

Heat the remaining oil in a frying pan, add the onions, garlic and peppers and sauté for about 10 minutes until softening. Add the pepper mixture to the tomatoes and simmer, covered, for 45 minutes until very soft. Taste and season with salt and pepper.

Preheat a grill or barbecue. Sprinkle the steaks with olive oil and arrange on a rack over a foil-lined grill pan. Grill for about 2 minutes on each side until crusty on the outside and still pink in the middle. Alternatively, barbecue over hot coals for slightly less time. Serve with the peperonata, which can be served hot or cold.

1 kg monkfish tail

olive oil, for brushing

sea salt and freshly ground
black pepper

niçoise sauce

200 g canned tomatoes
or 6 fresh tomatoes,
skinned and deseeded

2 garlic cloves, crushed

2 tablespoons olive oil

125 ml white wine

250 ml fish stock

leaves from 2–3 sprigs of
thyme, chopped

leaves from 2–3 small sprigs
of tarragon, chopped

2 fresh sage leaves

1 bay leaf

sea salt and freshly ground
black pepper

to serve

12 black olives, pitted
and chopped

fennel fronds

an instant-read meat
thermometer (optional)

serves 4

carbohydrate 2 g

This classic dish is usually made with a whole, large monkfish tail, but cutlets or even four smaller, individual tails may be used instead. The Niçoise sauce has a delicous herby flavour, while the black olives and fennel fronds add a splash of colour to the dish.

roast gigot of monkfish
with niçoise sauce

To make the Niçoise sauce, put the tomatoes, garlic and oil in a saucepan, bring to the boil, reduce the heat and simmer until they cook to a pulp – crush them from time to time. Add the wine and keep simmering until it has been absorbed by the tomatoes. Add the stock, thyme, tarragon, sage, bay leaf, salt and pepper.

Peel the skin off the monkfish and cut away the loose membrane. Shorten the tail with scissors but do not cut into the flesh or it will shrink back and expose the bone as it cooks. Brush the fish with the oil and season with salt and pepper.

Spoon half the sauce into a roasting tin, rest the fish on it and roast in a preheated oven at 180°C (350°F) Gas 4 for 10 minutes. Turn the fish over and cook for a further 10 minutes or until an instant-read thermometer registers 60°C (135°F). Transfer the fish to a serving dish and keep it warm.

Pour the roasting juices back into the saucepan of Niçoise sauce, bring to the boil and simmer until reduced to a pulp. Add salt and pepper to taste.

Pour the sauce around the fish, add the olives and fennel fronds and serve.

neapolitan seafood stew

This wholesome soup-stew is a great low-carb dish for any time of year. In Naples, it's made with whatever fish is available at the fish market so feel free to alter the composition of this recipe according to what's available in your local market, but make sure you include thick white fish, shellfish and crustacea, such as prawns.

4 large garlic cloves, crushed

1 bunch of thyme or rosemary

12 live clams or other bivalves

12 live mussels, well scrubbed

4 tablespoons olive oil

2 large onions, cut into wedges through the root

8 ripe, very red tomatoes, skinned, halved and deseeded

1 kg thick boneless white fish fillets, such as cod

4–8 small whole fish, cleaned and scaled (optional)

8 uncooked prawns

1 litre boiling fish stock

sea salt and freshly ground black pepper

serves 4

carbohydrate 16 g

Put 250 ml water in a saucepan with 1 crushed garlic clove and half the herbs, bring to the boil, then simmer to extract the flavours. Add the clams, cover with a lid and cook at high heat, shaking the pan from time to time. Remove them as they open (about 1 minute) and put on a plate so they don't overcook. Add the mussels, cover with a lid and cook until they open. Remove as they do so and add to the clams.

Taste the cooking stock, and if not too gritty, strain it through coffee filters into a cup and set aside.

Heat the oil in a large frying pan, add the onion wedges and cook until lightly browned on both sides. Reduce the heat and cook until softened. Stir in the remaining garlic and cook for a few minutes until golden. Add lots of pepper, then the tomatoes, remaining herbs, both kinds of fish and the prawns. Pour in the stock and heat just to boiling point. Reduce the heat and simmer for a few minutes until the fish turns opaque.

Add the mussels, clams and the strained mussel poaching liquid, if using. Reheat and season to taste. Divide among 4 big soup bowls and serve immediately.

1 kg fresh ripe red tomatoes or 500 g canned Italian plum tomatoes

4 tablespoons olive oil

2 large onions, finely chopped

3 red peppers, peeled with a vegetable peeler, deseeded and chopped

6 garlic cloves, crushed with a pinch of salt

a large bunch of flat leaf parsley, chopped, big stalks reserved

500 ml fish stock or water

500 ml red wine, such as Zinfandel

a large sprig of thyme

2 fresh bay leaves

1 teaspoon dried chilli flakes

500 g clams

500 g mussels, well scrubbed

12 shelled large uncooked prawns, with tails

500 g shelled scallops, halved through their thickness if very large

sea salt and freshly ground black pepper

a handful of basil, to serve

serves 4

carbohydrate 29 g

All fishing communities have their version of fish stew or soup, using fish they are unable to sell at the market, such as unpopular varieties or undersized fish. Cioppino is the creation of Italian fisherfolk in San Francisco and nowadays uses delicious shellfish – far from the unsaleable fish of the past. It also includes Californian Zinfandel, though older recipes sometimes use white wine.

cioppino

To prepare fresh tomatoes, cut a cross in the bottom, then put in a bowl of boiling water. Remove after 10–30 seconds and slip off the skins. Working over a sieve set over a bowl to catch the juices, cut the tomatoes in half and deseed into the sieve. Chop the tomatoes and set aside. Push the juices through the sieve with the back of a spoon. If using canned tomatoes, do the same.

Heat the oil in a large flameproof casserole over low heat. Add the onions and peppers and cook slowly for 5 minutes. Add the garlic and continue simmering until the onions have softened, about 15–20 minutes. If you cover the pot, the onions will soften quicker.

Bruise the parsley stalks, then add them to the casserole with the fish stock, wine, tomatoes and their juices, thyme, bay leaves and chilli flakes and bring to the boil over high heat. Reduce the heat and simmer for about 30 minutes. The soup base can be held at this point until ready to serve. If you want to prepare in advance, cool and refrigerate until next day.

When ready to serve, put about 3 cm water in a large saucepan, add the clams and mussels, in batches if necessary, and bring to the boil with the lid on. Remove them as they open – try not to overcook, or they will be tough. Discard any shells that don't open. Strain the cooking liquid to remove any grit, then add to the soup base.

Bring the soup base to the boil, reduce the heat, add the prawns and scallops and cook for about 1 minute just until opaque. Add the reserved clams and mussels, reheat for about 1 minute, season to taste, then stir in the chopped parsley. Serve in a tureen or in soup bowls. Tear basil over the top and serve.

poultry and meat

bangkok chicken

2 tablespoons groundnut or sunflower oil

4 skinless chicken breasts, about 800 g, quartered crossways

150 ml chicken stock

500 ml canned coconut milk

125 g pea aubergines* or chopped cucumber

1 teaspoon Thai fish sauce or 1 teaspoon sea salt

freshly squeezed juice of 1 lime

a large bunch of fresh Thai basil (page 123) or mint

green curry paste

5–6 fresh green chillies, deseeded and sliced

a small bunch of fresh coriander, chopped

2 stalks of lemongrass, trimmed and thinly sliced

3 cm fresh ginger, peeled and thinly sliced

3 cm fresh galangal, peeled and sliced (optional)

4 fresh kaffir lime leaves, shredded hair-thin

2 teaspoons coriander seeds, crushed

1 teaspoon cumin seeds, crushed

4 spring onions or small red onions, chopped

4 garlic cloves, crushed

serves 4

carbohydrate 5 g

Thai cooks use incendiary amounts of chillies, often the blindingly hot bird's eye chillies, but for Western palates the quantity has been reduced. The green curry paste makes double the amount you'll need, so store the extra in the fridge to use in other dishes. You can buy ready-made paste, but check the label for sugar or any other high-carb ingredients. Serve this classic curry with one or more vegetable dishes.

Put all the green curry paste ingredients in a food processor and process until smooth. Alternatively, use a mortar and pestle. Set aside half the mixture for this recipe and refrigerate or freeze the rest.

Heat the groundnut oil in a large, preferably non-stick, frying pan or wok, add the chicken and sauté for 2–3 minutes or until firm and golden. Using tongs, turn the pieces over as they cook.

Stir in the reserved green curry paste and sauté, stirring constantly, for about 1 minute. Add the chicken stock and bring to the boil.

Add half the coconut milk and the pea aubergines and cook, covered, at a rapid simmer (not a boil) for 5 minutes. Using tongs, turn the chicken pieces over, then reduce the heat to a very gentle simmer. Add the remaining coconut milk and the fish sauce and cook, uncovered, for a further 8–12 minutes.

Add the lime juice and sprinkle with Thai basil or mint. Transfer to 4 soup bowls and serve immediately.

Note Pea aubergines, like bunches of green mini-grapes, are sold in Thai and Asian stores. If you can't find them, just leave them out.

In this easy, minimal, but classic Japanese dish, sake is used to add sweetness and flavour and act as a tenderizer, while salt adds balance to the taste. The chicken breasts are often skewered with three bamboo satay sticks in the shape of a fan: it stabilizes them for even cooking and looks elegant. Do not overcook the chicken: grill for 12 minutes at the most.

japanese salt-grilled chicken

4 boneless, skinless
chicken breasts

3 tablespoons sake
or dry sherry

sea salt

to serve

4 spring onions
Japanese pink pickled ginger

*12 bamboo satay sticks, soaked in
water for 30 minutes*

serves 4

carbohydrate 1 g

Put each chicken breast between 2 sheets of foil. Using your hand, a meat mallet or a rolling pin, pound and flatten them to about half the original thickness. Transfer to a glass or ceramic dish and pour over the sake, turn the chicken to coat and set aside for about 5–10 minutes to tenderize.

Remove the chicken from the dish and push 3 bamboo satay sticks through the length of each breast to hold them flat.

Sprinkle a layer of salt over both sides of each piece of chicken. Put each piece onto a sheet of foil and cook under a preheated hot grill or over hot coals on a barbecue for 4–5 minutes, about 5 cm from the heat. Turn the chicken over and cook for a further 2–4 minutes. The chicken must be golden brown, cooked right through, but not dry.

Eat hot, warm or cold with a spring onion and a pile of pink pickled ginger.

lao chicken and ginger

in coconut milk

2–4 tablespoons groundnut or sunflower oil

6 shallots or 4 onions, sliced

5 cm fresh ginger, sliced and finely chopped

3–6 garlic cloves, crushed

8–12 chicken thighs, with skin

2 medium-hot chillies, red or green, cored and sliced, plus extra to serve

1 tablespoon Thai fish sauce, or 1 teaspoon shrimp paste (blachan or belacan; page 102), toasted in a dry frying pan or the oven

500 ml coconut milk

250 g pea aubergines (optional; page 139)

6 spring onions, halved then thinly sliced lengthways

10 large coriander sprigs

serves 4

carbohydrate 10 g

A traditional dish from Laos, this is usually made with a whole chicken. This recipe, however, just uses chicken thighs to enable it to be served more easily. The cooling coconut milk, stirred in to counteract the heat of the chillies, the fish sauce, ginger and garlic identify this unmistakably as a dish of the East.

Heat the oil in a wok, add the shallots and stir-fry until golden. Add the ginger and garlic and stir-fry for 1–2 minutes. Remove to a plate, then add the chicken to the wok, and fry on all sides until golden. Stir in the onion mixture, chillies and fish sauce or shrimp paste.

Add the coconut milk, bring it gently to the boil (stirring, or it will curdle), then reduce the heat and simmer until the chicken is tender.

Add the pea aubergines, simmer for 2 minutes, then serve topped with spring onions, coriander and chillies.

This dish is quick to make if you get your butcher to cut up the chicken, and the flavour of tarragon lifts it out of the ordinary. Make this dish midweek and you'll have a lovely supper on the table in under an hour, or serve it for your next dinner party and your friends will think you slaved away all day.

chicken with tarragon

1 tablespoon unsalted butter

1 tablespoon sunflower oil

1 free-range corn-fed chicken, about 2 kg, cut into 6–8 pieces

2 carrots, chopped

1 shallot or ½ small onion, chopped

a sprig of thyme

2–3 sprigs of flat leaf parsley

a bunch of tarragon

3 tablespoons crème fraîche

sea salt and freshly ground black pepper

serves 4

carbohydrate 5 g

Heat the butter and oil in a large sauté pan with a lid. Add the chicken pieces and cook until brown, about 5 minutes. Work in batches if your pan is not big enough. Put the browned chicken pieces on a plate and season well with salt and pepper.

Add the carrots and shallot to the pan and cook, stirring for a minute or so. Return the chicken to the pan and add water to cover half-way. Add the thyme, parsley and a few sprigs of tarragon. Cover and simmer gently for 30 minutes.

Meanwhile, strip the leaves from the remaining tarragon, chop them finely and set aside. Add the stems to the cooking chicken.

Remove the chicken from the pan and put in a serving dish. Remove and discard the tarragon stems. (The recipe can be prepared a few hours in advance up to this point, then completed just before serving.)

Raise the heat and cook the sauce until reduced by half. Strain and return the sauce to the pan. Stir in the crème fraîche and the chopped tarragon. Heat briefly (do not boil) and pour over the chicken. Serve immediately.

These little birds are easy to serve at a dinner when there is not much time for cooking. They take just over 30 minutes in the oven, and the juices make a delicious and simple gravy. When available, use the bones of a roast chicken to make stock. Or you can use fresh stock from the supermarket, if more convenient. Serve with a simple fresh salad.

spatchcocked poussins
with rosemary and lemon glaze

4–6 poussins
1 tablespoon freshly squeezed lemon juice
1 tablespoon unsalted butter
1 tablespoon chopped fresh flat leaf parsley
sea salt and freshly ground black pepper

marinade

30 g unsalted butter
2 tablespoons extra virgin olive oil
2 teaspoons grated lemon zest
a sprig of rosemary
2 garlic cloves, sliced
5 tablespoons white wine

serves 4–6

carbohydrate 0 g

To prepare the marinade, put the butter, olive oil, lemon zest, rosemary, garlic and wine in a saucepan and bring to the boil. Remove from the heat and let cool.

Put each bird breast side down on a work surface. Using kitchen scissors, cut along either side of the backbones and remove them.

Put the bones in a large saucepan, cover with cold water, bring to the boil and simmer for 30 minutes. Lift out the bones with tongs and boil down the stock to about 250 ml. Set aside.

Meanwhile, turn the birds breast side up and flatten the breastbones until you hear them crack. Flatten the birds further, folding the legs inward. Set them side-by-side in a roasting tin and sprinkle with salt and pepper. Pour over the marinade and transfer the tin to the refrigerator until 30 minutes or so before you start to cook.

Roast in the middle of a preheated oven at 240°C (475°F) Gas 8 for 35–40 minutes. Baste the birds with the juices after 20 minutes. When they are cooked, lift them onto a serving dish, stir the lemon juice into the pan juices, then stir in the stock, butter and parsley. Taste and adjust the seasoning with salt and pepper, then serve.

chettinad chicken

8 large dried red chillies

2 tablespoons coriander seeds, toasted in a dry frying pan

1 onion, finely chopped

3 cm fresh ginger, peeled and grated

4 skinless boneless chicken breasts, cut into chunks

3 tomatoes, chopped

2 teaspoons tamarind paste

tarka spice-fry

2 tablespoons groundnut oil or ghee

¼ teaspoon ground turmeric

4 black peppercorns

¼ teaspoon fennel seeds

¼ teaspoon cumin seeds

a few curry leaves (optional) (see page 121)

to serve

a handful of coriander leaves, chopped (optional)

2–4 green chillies, halved and deseeded (optional)

natural yoghurt

serves 4

carbohydrate 7 g

This traditional Indian dish uses the perfect low-carb ingredient – chicken breasts. This is not a dish for the faint-hearted, since it's made with lots of dried chillies and served with even more fresh ones. The ground chillies and roasted coriander seeds add both fire and aroma. Tamarind is sold as a paste or in blocks. If you can't find it, add the juice of a small lemon.

Using a mortar and pestle, blender or spice mill, grind the dried chillies and coriander seeds to a fine powder. Set aside.

To make the tarka spice-fry, put the oil in a frying pan and heat well. Add the turmeric, peppercorns, fennel and cumin seeds and curry leaves, if using. Let sizzle briefly, then add the onion. Sauté for a few minutes, then add the ginger. Sauté for a further 6 minutes or so, until the onion is soft. If necessary, add a dash of water to prevent the mixture sticking to the pan.

Add the chicken and toss well to coat with the tarka. Sauté until the chicken begins to brown. Add enough water to cover, about 325 ml, then the tomatoes. Bring to the boil, reduce the heat and gently simmer until the chicken is cooked, about 8–10 minutes.

A few minutes before the end of cooking time, stir in about 1¼ tablespoons of the reserved ground chile-coriander spice blend, to taste. Put the tamarind paste in a bowl, add a ladle of liquid, stir to dissolve, then stir into the pan.* Sprinkle with the coriander and top with the chillies, if using, then serve with yoghurt as an accompaniment.

*Variation If you would like a thicker sauce, at this point, transfer the pieces of chicken to a plate and keep them warm. Bring the liquid to the boil and simmer until reduced and thickened. Return the chicken to the pan, turn to coat, reheat, then serve.

4 chicken legs (thigh and drumstick)

lemon or lime wedges, to serve

jerk seasoning paste

3–4 habanero chillies, deseeded

1 teaspoon chopped fresh thyme

3 garlic cloves, coarsely chopped

1 bay leaf

1 teaspoon allspice berries (about 20)

¼ teaspoon freshly grated nutmeg

3 spring onions, chopped

2 plum tomatoes, skinned (fresh or canned)

freshly squeezed juice of ½ lime

80 ml groundnut oil

½ teaspoon salt

an instant-read meat thermometer (optional)

serves 4

carbohydrate 0 g

There are as many jerk chicken recipes in Jamaica as there are cooks, but all include the fiery Scotch bonnet chilli or the closely related habanero chile, plus a good dose of native allspice. Jerk seasoning also includes nutmeg, a native of the Spice Islands of Indonesia, grown in the West Indies since the 19th century. Traditionally grilled over wood, jerk chicken – or pork – can easily be cooked on the barbecue or in the oven.

jerk chicken

To make the jerk seasoning paste, grind the ingredients to a smooth paste with a mortar and pestle.

Cut slashes in the chicken legs and spread with half the jerk seasoning paste. Rub the paste all over and into the slashes, cover and marinate in the refrigerator for at least 2 hours or overnight.

Put the chicken legs skin side down in a roasting tin. Roast in a preheated oven at 200°C (400°F) Gas 6 for 40–45 minutes or until crisp and cooked through, turning halfway through the cooking time and coating with the remaining marinade.

To cook on a barbecue, preheat a charcoal grill until very hot. Cook the chicken over high heat to begin with, then adjust the rack further away from the fire as soon as the surfaces of the chicken have begun to brown. Cook for 15–20 minutes or until done, turning frequently and basting with the remaining marinade. You must cook poultry thoroughly so there is no pink inside: if you have an instant-read thermometer, it should read 75°C (165°F) when inserted into the thickest part of the thigh. Serve hot with lemon or lime wedges.

Chinese red-cooking involves poaching meat, poultry, game or even fish in a dark, soy-based sauce. When the sauce is spiced with star anise, cinnamon and, sometimes, additional spices from the five-spice brigade, it is used as a 'master sauce'. This is then used like a stock, cooked first as in the recipe below, then stored for later use. When it has been used a few times, it is considered mature and more desirable.

red-cooked chicken legs

150 ml dark soy sauce

3 tablespoons Chinese rice wine or dry sherry

2 thin slices of fresh ginger

3 cinnamon sticks, halved

5 whole star anise

2 whole cloves

3 spring onions

½ teaspoon grated orange or lemon zest

1 tablespoon freshly squeezed lemon juice

½ teaspoon sugar

4 large chicken legs (thighs and drumsticks)

serves 4

carbohydrate 7 g

Put the soy sauce and rice wine in a saucepan and add 1 litre water. Add the ginger, cinnamon, star anise, cloves, spring onions, orange zest, lemon juice and sugar. Bring to the boil and turn off the heat. Leave for at least 10 minutes to infuse the flavours.

Add the chicken legs and bring to the boil. Reduce the heat and simmer for 40 minutes, or until cooked through and tender.

Transfer the legs to a serving bowl or plate and spoon over some of the sauce. Alternatively, use a Chinese cleaver to chop them into bite-sized pieces. Transfer any remaining sauce to an airtight container and refrigerate or freeze for later use.

rolled turkey breast

with spinach, bacon and cheese

a small boneless breast of
turkey, about 550 g

250 g cooked chopped spinach

freshly grated nutmeg

4 slices of back bacon

250 g Cheddar or Gruyère
cheese, thinly sliced

2 tablespoons olive or
sunflower oil

sea salt and freshly ground
black pepper

herb gravy

300 ml chicken stock

175 g unsalted butter

1 tablespoon chopped fresh flat
leaf parsley

2 teaspoons chopped
fresh tarragon

kitchen string

*an instant-read meat
thermometer (optional)*

serves 4

carbohydrate 1 g

Poultry, cheese and bacon are all suitable for a low-carb diet and combine well in this attractive dish. Stuffed turkey meat can often be dry, but with a juicy filling and buttery herb gravy, it's transformed into a deliciously moist dish. Serve with vegetables, such as Braised Celery with Lardons and Anchovies (page 209) or Roast Butternut Squash with Garlic and Thyme (page 204) for special occasions.

Put the turkey breast skin side down on a flat board and hit it 2–3 times with the side of a heavy cleaver or meat mallet to flatten it. Cut a horizontal slice off the thickest part of the breast to even it up more, and use it to cover a thinner part. Season the turkey with salt and pepper and season the spinach with plenty of nutmeg.

Overlap the bacon slices to cover the inside surface of the meat and cover this with the spinach. Make a third layer with slices of cheese. Roll up the turkey into a roll and tie it neatly with kitchen string. Brush it all over with the oil. Roast in the middle of a preheated oven at 200°C (400°F) Gas 6 for 1 hour or until an instant-read thermometer measures 82°C (180°F). Baste the turkey frequently with some of the stock for the herb gravy.

When the turkey is done, remove from the oven and transfer to a serving dish. Remove and discard the string. Reserve any roasting juices and any more that collect in the serving dish.

To make the gravy, put the butter, remaining stock, parsley and tarragon in a saucepan and bring to the boil. Add the juices from the roasting tin and the serving dish.

Slice the turkey crossways and serve with the herb gravy.

175 g Puy lentils

½ teaspoon dried thyme or 2 sprigs fresh, chopped

1 bay leaf

2 tablespoons olive oil or melted butter

6 small onions, peeled

3 carrots, diced

150 g or 6 slices of back bacon

2 guinea fowl

2 tablespoons brandy or Calvados

500 ml chicken stock

2 teaspoons chopped fresh tarragon

12 chipolata sausages, preferably made with venison (optional)

sea salt

an instant-read meat thermometer (optional)

serves 6

carbohydrate 42 g

Guinea fowl are farmed game birds and are available all year round. They are low in fat and calories, but high in protein. Here they are flamed in brandy and then cooked on a bed of vegetables with chipolata sausages. Tiny, dark Puy lentils originate from Le Puy in France and are a favourite with cooks. If unavailable, use other brown lentils.

guinea fowl with puy lentils

Rinse the lentils well, put in a saucepan, add the thyme, bay leaf and a little salt, then cover them with 1 litre water. Cook until soft and the water has been absorbed, adding more water during the cooking if they dry out before becoming tender.

Heat the oil in a roasting tin on top of the stove, add the onions, carrots and bacon, fry until browned and remove to a plate. Add the guinea fowl to the tin and brown them on all sides, sprinkling them with a little salt, then pour the brandy over them. Stand back and ignite it. When the flames have gone out, return the vegetables and bacon to the tin and tuck them around the guinea fowl. Add the stock and half the tarragon, then roast in a preheated oven at 170°C (325°F) Gas 3 for 1½ hours or until an instant-read thermometer registers 80°C (175°F). Put the chipolatas, if using, in the tin for the last 20 minutes of cooking time.

Lift the guinea fowl and chipolatas, if using, onto a platter and cut the birds into 6 portions each. Keep them warm. Bring the vegetables and stock to the boil, add the lentils and the rest of the tarragon and ladle onto a serving dish or 6 heated dinner plates. Arrange the guinea fowl on top and serve with the chipolata sausages, if using.

Salade tiède or warm salad is one of the classics of French cooking. It includes bitter leaves such as spinach, frisée and escarole, and the salad is topped with crisp bacon, in this case the French lardons. The cooking juices from the pine nuts, garlic and bacon are used to dress the salad. Without the duck, it can be served as a first course or side dish.

warm french duck salad

4 duck breasts

2 tablespoons olive oil, plus extra for brushing

500 g baby spinach leaves

100 g pine nuts

3 garlic cloves, thinly sliced

250 g bacon lardons, pancetta cubes or thinly sliced smoked pancetta, as fatty as possible

red wine vinaigrette

4 tablespoons extra virgin olive oil

2 teaspoons red wine vinegar

sea salt and freshly ground black pepper

serves 4–8

carbohydrate 3 g

Put the duck breasts skin side down in a frying pan lightly brushed with olive oil. Sprinkle the flesh side with a little sea salt. Cook gently over low heat for 20–30 minutes to render out the fat – you will have to pour it off from time to time into a heatproof bowl. Take it slowly – the skin will gradually become crisp and golden and the fat line will almost disappear.

Meanwhile, make the vinaigrette. Put the oil, vinegar, salt and pepper in a bowl and beat with a fork or small whisk.

Turn the duck over and cook at high heat just to brown the flesh side – the interior should remain rare. Remove from the pan and let rest for about 5 minutes if serving hot, or 20 minutes if serving cool. Carve crossways on a wooden board, making sure each slice has its share of crackling.

Put the spinach in a bowl, add the vinaigrette and toss lightly. Divide the leaves among 4 dinner plates or 8 starter plates.

Meanwhile, rinse and dry the frying pan. Reheat, add 2 tablespoons olive oil, then the pine nuts. Toast over low heat, tossing gently, until golden on all sides, about 1 minute. Take care – they burn easily. Remove from the pan and let cool on a plate. Add the garlic to the pan and fry gently until crisp and golden brown. Remove to the same plate.

Add the bacon lardons and fry gently until crispy. Add the lardons to the salads, top with the pine nuts and garlic, then spoon the hot scented oil from the pan over the salads. Place the duck on top of the salad, sprinkle with black pepper and serve.

Duck with olives is a classic Mediterranean dish. Instead of using a whole duck, cut into pieces, this recipe uses 'magrets' or boneless breast portions. The skin is left on but is slashed to enable it to brown well and allow some of the duck fat to add richness to the sauce. Choose green olives, unpitted or ready-stuffed, perhaps with anchovies, lemon zest or chilli.

spanish duck with olives

2 large magrets (boneless breast portions) of muscovy or other duck, about 500 g

4 garlic cloves, finely chopped then crushed

8 shallots or pearl onions

6 tablespoons aged sweet sherry, such as Pedro Ximenez, or 4 tablespoons pomegranate molasses

40 whole, or pitted and stuffed green olives (with anchovies, lemon zest or almonds)

4 tablespoons chicken or beef consommé, or rich stock

400 g cooked (or canned) white beans, lentils or chickpeas, drained

2 tablespoons fresh herbs, such as parsley and celery tops

sea salt and freshly ground black pepper

a ridged stove-top grill pan

serves 4

carbohydrate 24 g

Preheat a ridged stove-top grill pan until very hot. Pat the duck breasts dry with kitchen paper.

Mix 1 teaspoon pepper, ½ teaspoon salt and half of the garlic to a paste. Rub some all over the duck breasts. Make 3 diagonal slashes on the skin side of each breast, then cook, skin side down, for 2 minutes. Reduce the heat to moderate and continue to cook until the fat runs and the surface is darkly browned.

Pour out and reserve the fat, returning 1 tablespoon to the pan. Using tongs, turn the duck breasts over. Add the shallots and sherry. Cover and cook over low heat for a further 4–6 minutes or until the duck is rare or medium-rare, depending on your taste.

Add the olives and another tablespoon of duck fat to the sauce. Remove the duck breasts and keep them warm. Add the consommé to the pan, then shake and stir the pan contents until the sauce becomes a rich syrupy glaze.

Put the beans in a saucepan and crush coarsely with a fork or potato masher. Stir in 2 tablespoons of the duck fat, salt, pepper, herbs and the remaining garlic and heat through.

Cut the duck crossways or diagonally into 5-mm slices. Serve with a trickle of sauce and a mound of the mashed beans.

Make sure the meat is at room temperature before you cook it – if taken straight from the fridge to the grill, the outside will be cooked long before the inside has come up to temperature. The peppery flavour of the rocket perfectly complements the rich juicy steak. A good side dish to accompany this would be Grilled and Sautéed Mushrooms (page 200).

beefsteak with rocket

4 T-bone steaks, about 200 g each

2 tablespoons olive oil

200 g wild rocket

sea salt and freshly ground black pepper

chopped fresh parsley, to serve

a ridged stove-top grill pan

serves 4

carbohydrate 1 g

Brush the steaks with olive oil and season well with salt and pepper. Heat a ridged stove-top grill pan or light a barbecue. When the pan is smoking hot, add the steaks and cook for 2 minutes on each side to seal, then lower the heat and continue to cook for about 4 minutes per side for medium-rare steaks, less for rare.

Transfer the steaks to a chopping board, cut the meat from the bone, and slice it thickly. Put a pile of rocket on 4 warm plates and arrange the sliced meat on top. Pour any juices from the steaks onto the meat and serve immediately, topped with chopped parsley.

Choosing the right steak for grilling or barbecuing is the first step to producing the perfect steak. As its name suggests, rib eye steak is the 'eye' of the rib roast and is marbled with fat, giving a moist result. It has a good flavour and is not too huge.

rib eye steak
with anchovy butter

125 g butter, softened

8 anchovy fillets in oil, drained and coarsely chopped

2 tablespoons chopped fresh parsley

4 rib eye steaks, about 250 g each

sea salt and freshly ground black pepper

a ridged stove-top grill pan

serves 4

carbohydrate 0 g

Put the butter, anchovies, parsley and a little pepper in a bowl and beat well. Transfer to a sheet of foil and roll up into a log. Chill until required.

Season the steaks with salt and pepper, then heat a ridged stove-top grill pan or preheat a barbecue to high and brush the grill rack with oil. When the pan is smoking hot, add the steaks and cook for 3 minutes on each side for rare, 4–5 minutes for medium and 5–6 minutes for well done.

Transfer the steaks to a warmed serving plate and put 2 slices of anchovy butter on each one. Let rest for about 5 minutes before serving in order to set the juices.

Beef loin is often prepared by a butcher ready to be sliced into steaks, but it can be bought in a whole piece and is the easiest cut to carve. The meat is very tender and, except for the outside, is free from fat. This is a great choice if you're catering for friends or family who aren't following a low-carb diet.

roast boned beef loin
basted with red wine gravy

1.5 kg strip loin of beef (boned sirloin, without the undercut)

3 garlic cloves, sliced

6 small tip sprigs of thyme

100 g unsalted butter

2 onions, sliced

125 ml red wine

sea salt and freshly ground black pepper

an instant-read meat thermometer (optional)

serves 6

carbohydrate 4 g

Trim off a sheet of fat from the top of the meat and keep it to use as a cushion under the roast. Make 6 slits in the underside of the meat and push in a sliver of garlic and a sprig of thyme. Season with the salt and pepper and spread half the butter generously over the underside of the meat. Set the fat in the roasting pan and put the sliced onions on top. Add the sirloin and roast in a preheated oven at 220°C (425°F) Gas 7 for 20 minutes.

Pour the wine into the pan, let it bubble for a moment, then spoon it over the beef. Continue to cook the meat until it is done to your liking, preferably pink, or when an instant-read thermometer registers 65°C (150°F). Base the meat frequently, adding water to the pan when the wine becomes low.

Transfer the meat to a carving platter and let rest it in a warm place for 10 minutes.

To make a light gravy, add 25 ml water to the roasting tin and stir it through the reduced wine. Stir in the remaining butter to make a sauce. Strain into a saucepan, bring to the boil, then add salt and pepper to taste. Serve in a separate sauceboat.

1 kg loin of veal or turkey breast
600 ml dry white wine
1 celery stick, chopped
1 carrot, chopped
1 small onion, chopped
1 bay leaf
3 cloves

tuna mayonnaise

200 g canned tuna in oil, drained
6 anchovy fillets in oil, rinsed
1 tablespoon capers, rinsed, plus extra to serve
2 hard-boiled egg yolks
300 ml olive oil
freshly squeezed juice of 1 lemon
2 teaspoons white wine vinegar
sea salt and freshly ground black pepper

to serve

thin lemon slices
a few parsley sprigs

kitchen string

serves 6–8

carbohydrate 3 g

This is one of the most famous dishes to come out of Piedmont in Italy and is still a favourite. It can also be made with turkey instead of veal, if you prefer, and if cooked and cooled in the poaching liquid, it will remain moist. Although it takes a bit of time to prepare, the dish is served cold and so can be made well ahead of time.

veal with tuna mayonnaise sauce

Two days before serving, put the veal or turkey in a bowl with the wine, celery, carrot, onion, bay leaf and cloves, mix well and let marinate in the refrigerator for 24 hours.

Remove the meat from the marinade and tie up neatly with fine string. If using turkey, remove the skin. Put in a saucepan just large enough to hold it. Pour in the marinade, then top up with water until the meat is just covered. Cover with a lid, bring to a boil, then reduce the heat and simmer very slowly for about 1¼ hours or until cooked through. When cooked, remove from the heat and let cool in the liquid.

When cold, remove the meat from the liquid, wrap and chill the meat, and strain the liquid. Chill the liquid for a couple of hours to set any grease. Lift off and discard any grease and set the liquid aside.

To make the tuna mayonnaise, put the tuna, anchovies, capers and hard-boiled egg yolks in a blender or food processor and blend until smooth. With the machine running, pour in the olive oil in a thin stream until it has all been absorbed and the is mixture thick and homogenized. Scrape out into a bowl and season to taste with the lemon juice and vinegar.

Using the poaching liquid, carefully dilute the sauce until it is the right flowing consistency. Taste and adjust the seasoning with salt and pepper. Slice the veal or turkey thinly. Spread a few tablespoons of the sauce on a large, flat serving dish. Add a layer of veal, coat with the sauce and continue until all is used up, ending with sauce. Sprinkle some extra capers on top, add the slices of lemon and a few parsley sprigs and serve immediately.

4 lamb shanks

2 tablespoons olive oil

tex-mex spices*

½ teaspoon garlic powder

½ teaspoon ground red chilli

½ teaspoon dried oregano

½ teaspoon chilli flakes

1 teaspoon sea salt

½ teaspoon freshly ground black pepper

sauce

1 tablespoon olive oil

2 garlic cloves, crushed

2 teaspoons hot oak-smoked paprika

1 teaspoon ground cumin

1 tablespoon red wine vinegar

6 beef or large tomatoes, skinned, halved and deseeded

2 tablespoons chopped fresh mint

½ teaspoon sugar

sea salt and freshly ground black pepper

serves 4

carbohydrate 9 g

Lamb shanks are very popular these days and most butchers and supermarkets sell them. When slow-roasted like this, they are much more tender than the equivalent shin of beef. This unusual recipe pairs them with Tex-Mex spices and a spicy tomato and mint sauce. Serve with green vegetables, such as French Beans with Garlic (page 180).

slow-roasted lamb shanks
with tex-mex spices

Brush the shanks with the olive oil. Put the garlic powder, ground red chilli, oregano, chilli flakes, salt and pepper in a bowl, mix well, then sprinkle over the shanks.

Set the shanks end to end in a roasting tin. Put in the middle of a preheated oven and cook at at 150°C (300°F) Gas 2 for 2 hours, turning them over 2–3 times. Remove from the oven and let rest for 30 minutes.

To make the sauce, heat the oil in a large pan, add the garlic and cook to a light brown (it will give off a delicious roasting aroma). Add the paprika and cumin and cook for 1 minute without letting them burn. Pour in the vinegar, then add the tomatoes, breaking them up with a wooden spoon and cooking to form a lumpy sauce. Add the mint, season with salt and pepper and add sugar to taste.

Dish up the shanks, pour off any excess fat and add 2–3 tablespoons water to the tin to make a little stock. Stir well, then add it to the sauce. Bring to the boil, then season with salt and pepper and add more sugar if necessary. Pour the sauce over the meat and serve.

*Note Many supermarkets sell ready-made Tex-Mex spice mixes. Use 1½ tablespoons and mix with the salt.

This recipe is a magnificent way to cook lamb long and slowly. The black olives enrich the dish and give it a smoky taste. The cutlets can be finished off in a medium hot oven instead of cooking on top if you prefer. They are very good reheated.

braised lamb cutlets
with onions, herbs and olives

8–12 lamb cutlets, depending on size

100 ml olive oil

900 g onions, thinly sliced

2 tablespoons chopped fresh oregano and rosemary, mixed

4 anchovy fillets in oil, drained, rinsed and chopped

16 black olives, pitted

sea salt and freshly ground black pepper

rosemary sprigs, to serve

serves 4

carbohydrate 18 g

Season the meat on both sides with salt and pepper.

Heat half the oil in a large sauté pan until very hot, then add the cutlets and quickly brown on both sides. Remove to a plate and let cool.

Heat the remaining oil in the same pan and add the onions. Cook over gentle heat for 15 minutes, stirring occasionally, until the onions begin to soften – do not let them brown. Stir in the herbs, anchovies, olives, salt and pepper.

Arrange the cutlets on top of the bed of onions and cover with a lid. Cook over very low heat for 20 minutes, watching that the onions don't catch and burn. Serve topped with rosemary sprigs.

Without crackling to add texture, pork cries out for some form of flavouring – the loin is the ideal cut for such treatment. Ask your butcher to chine it by removing the backbone, or to cut it down between the ribs, so that you can carve it easily into chops. Gentle roasting gives ample time for the full flavour to develop.

slow-roasted pork loin
with rosemary, madeira and orange

1.5 kg centre loin of pork
200 ml Madeira wine
100 ml freshly squeezed orange juice
2 sprigs of rosemary, bruised
2 oranges, peeled and sliced into 4 slices each
sea salt and freshly ground black pepper

an instant-read meat thermometer (optional)

serves 4

carbohydrate 11 g

Score the fat with a criss cross pattern and season the meat with plenty of salt and pepper, rubbing it in well. Put a double thickness of kitchen foil in a large roasting tin and turn up the edges. Put in the meat fat side down and pour in the Madeira and juice. Add the rosemary. Leave for about 2 hours if possible, then put in the middle of a preheated oven at 170°C (325°F) Gas 3 and slow-roast for 1 hour.

Carefully turn the meat over, then add the orange slices and about 125 ml water if it is starting to dry out. Cook for a further 30 minutes. Then raise the oven temperature to 220°C (425°F) Gas 7 for a final 10 minutes or until an instant-read thermometer registers 80°C (175°F).

Lift the meat out onto a serving dish and arrange the orange slices around. Carefully pour the juices into a jug, then serve.

vegetables

Char-grilling produces a delicious flavour and this simple dish makes a tasty starter or side dish. Freshly grated Parmesan cheese, sea salt, aïoli, or some chilli oil mixed with rice vinegar are all perfect accompaniments.

char-grilled asparagus

olive oil, for brushing

1–3 asparagus spears per person

sea salt, to serve

a ridged stove-top grill pan

serves 1

carbohydrate 2 g

Brush a ridged stove-top grill pan with olive oil, add the asparagus spears and press down with a spatula. Cook for 2 minutes on each side (they should be barely cooked). Alternatively, cook in a microwave for about 2 minutes or in a steamer. Test for doneness (they should be quite firm and crisp), steam or microwave a little longer if necessary, then either serve immediately or plunge into iced water to stop the cooking. Drain, plunge again, then drain.

Arrange on a serving plate with the tips all one way and serve with salt for sprinkling.

When cooled, they can be kept, covered with clingfilm, for 1–2 hours before serving.

French beans are the classic accompaniment for lamb, but they are equally nice with fish and chicken. Or you can serve them at room temperature, as part of a salad buffet. This recipe also works well with thin slices of steamed courgettes, sautéed with the garlic.

french beans with garlic

625 g small green beans, trimmed

2 tablespoons extra virgin olive oil

1 tablespoon unsalted butter

2 garlic cloves, crushed

a handful of flat leaf parsley, chopped

1 teaspoon freshly squeezed lemon juice (optional)

coarse sea salt and freshly ground black pepper

serves 4

carbohydrate 5 g

Bring a large saucepan of water to the boil. Add the beans and cook for 3–4 minutes. Drain and refresh under cold running water. Set aside.

Heat the oil and butter in a frying pan. Add the garlic, beans and salt, and cook on high for 1 minute, stirring. Remove from the heat and stir in the parsley and lemon juice, if using. Sprinkle with pepper and serve.

green vegetables

with lemon soy butter

8 baby courgettes or pattypans, green or yellow, halved lengthways

4 Chinese yard-long beans, cut into 10 cm lengths (optional)

100 g fine beans, stalks trimmed, points not

12 small asparagus tips

125 g shelled green peas, fresh or frozen

100 g sugar snap peas

100 g mangetouts, halved lengthways (optional)

lemon soy butter

125 g unsalted butter

6 spring onions, sliced crossways

3 cm fresh ginger, peeled and grated

1 teaspoon Japanese seven-spice (shichimi togarishi) or freshly ground black pepper

125 ml sake

freshly squeezed juice of 1–1½ lemons, about 125 ml

2 tablespoons Japanese soy sauce (shoyu)

serves 4

carbohydrate 17 g

Green vegetables, such as peas and beans, love steam and stay deliciously crunchy. Use any combination, according to what's available that day. Butter isn't a traditional ingredient in East and South-east Asia, but is now seen more and more. With lemon and soy, it makes a delicious dressing.

To make the lemon soy butter, put the butter into a saucepan, add the spring onions, ginger, seven-spice, sake, lemon juice and soy sauce, and heat gently. Set aside, but keep the mixture warm.

Put a steamer over boiling water, add the courgettes first and steam for about 1 minute. Add both kinds of beans and the asparagus tips and steam until all are tender but crisp. As each vegetable is done, transfer to a bowl of iced water to stop it cooking further.

Put the shelled peas into a small, heatproof bowl and add to the steamer. Add the sugar snaps and mangetouts, if using, and steam until just tender – as each is done, transfer to the bowl of iced water.

When all are done, drain in a colander, then put the colander into the steamer to reheat the vegetables, about 2 minutes. Transfer to a heated serving dish, pour over the lemon soy butter and serve as an accompaniment for other vegetable or meat dishes.

chinese greens

with star anise butter

Steaming is the perfect way to cook most leafy greens. They keep their nutrients and bright colour and need just a touch of spice to give them spark. Serve with a selection of other vegetable dishes, such as Chinese Mushrooms with Spring Onions and Sesame Seeds (page 203) or Roast Summer Vegetables (page 213) for a delicious vegetarian feast.

500 g Asian greens, such as Chinese broccoli, Chinese flowering cabbage or mustard cabbage, choi sum or baby pak choi, purple sprouting broccoli or broccoli florets, or regular cabbage, thickly sliced

star anise butter

3 whole star anise

125 g unsalted butter

½ teaspoon soy sauce, or to taste

1 tablespoon sesame oil

6 spring onions, trimmed and sliced crossways

serves 4

carbohydrate 4 g

Steam the chosen greens until just tender. Choy sum and pak choi will take about 4 minutes, or until the leaves are just wilted and the stems tender (take care not to overcook). Broccoli will take a few minutes longer.

Meanwhile, make the star anise butter. Put the star anise into small saucepan, add the butter, soy sauce, sesame oil and spring onions and melt over low heat. Alternatively, put into a bowl and microwave on HIGH for about 30 seconds. Set aside to infuse while the greens finish cooking.

To serve, transfer the greens to a plate, reheat the dressing, pour over the greens and serve.

Note If you're using any member of the cabbage family, don't cook it for more than about 7 minutes. After that time, it develops that infamous cabbagy smell. In any case, it will taste much nicer if it's still crunchy.

All parts of fennel are edible – the feathery leaves, the stalks and the bulb. It can be eaten raw or cooked in various ways, so it is a pity that so often this vegetable is just plainly boiled. Properly blanched for a short while, then roasted in butter, it is transformed into a perfect accompaniment for any roast, especially fish.

fennel roasted in butter

3 bulbs of Florence fennel

4 tablespoons olive oil or melted butter

sea salt

chopped dill, tarragon or fennel fronds (optional), to serve

serves 6

carbohydrate 2 g

Trim and remove the stalks and coarse outer leaves from the fennel if necessary. Cut each bulb in half, then each half into 2–3 pieces, depending on size. Slice each piece with a bit of stem or root attached to keep the pieces in place. Reserve any feathery fronds, to chop over the dish just before serving.

Put the fennel in a large saucepan of lightly salted water, bring to the boil and blanch until nearly tender. Drain and pat dry.

Arrange the pieces in a single layer in a roasting tin, baste with the oil or butter and cook in a preheated oven at 220°C (425°F) Gas 7 for about 20 minutes. From time to time, turn them and baste with the oil or butter so they brown evenly on all sides.

To enhance the aniseed flavour, dust with chopped dill, tarragon or fennel fronds, if using, then serve.

Variation Sprinkle with cheese and cook a further 5 minutes, then serve as a separate dish or starter.

Plum tomatoes are perfect for roasting as they have a low moisture content which means they retain their shape and have less tendency to burst. The garlic clove buried deep within each tomato softens to a creamy texture as it cooks and flavours the tomato's flesh.

roasted tomatoes
stuffed with garlic

6 large ripe plum or round tomatoes, preferably with stalks

6 small garlic cloves, peeled

1 tablespoon extra virgin olive oil

sea salt and freshly ground black pepper

a baking dish

serves 6

carbohydrate 5 g

Cut a thin sliver off the base of each tomato so it will stand upright. Cut off the tops and push a garlic clove deep inside each tomato. Season with salt and pepper and replace the tops.

Lightly oil a baking dish and add the tomatoes upright and close together. Sprinkle with olive oil and season again with salt and pepper. Bake in a preheated oven at 160°C (325°F) Gas 3 for about 2 hours, checking every now and then. They should be slightly shrivelled, and a brilliant red colour. Take them out and insert a sharp knife in the middle to see if the garlic clove is soft – it must be very soft. Replace the tops and serve hot or cold.

This is a very rich dish and deserves to be eaten on its own. If you like, you can add a layer of sliced hard-boiled eggs following the tomato sauce (which won't increase the carbohydrate content). This dish can be easily prepared in advance and then refrigerated, ready to put in the oven at a moment's notice.

baked aubergine, tomato, mozzarella and parmesan

4 medium aubergines

2 tablespoons olive oil, plus extra for the aubergines

1 small onion, finely chopped

800 g canned chopped tomatoes, drained

2 tablespoons chopped fresh basil

50–75 g freshly grated Parmesan cheese

200 g mozzarella cheese, thinly sliced

sea salt and freshly ground black pepper

a shallow oven dish, 25 cm diameter, lightly oiled

serves 4

carbohydrate 13 g

Cut the aubergines lengthways into strips 1.25 cm wide. Soak them for 30 minutes in a bowl of salted water.

Heat the oil in a frying pan, add the onion and cook for 5 minutes until softening, then add the tomatoes and basil and simmer gently for about 30 minutes. Season with salt and pepper.

Drain the aubergines, then rinse and pat dry. Shallow fry them or brush with olive oil and roast in a preheated oven at 180°C (350°F) Gas 4 for about 20 minutes until deep golden brown. Set aside.

Arrange the aubergines in a single layer in the oven dish, then add a layer of grated Parmesan, followed by a layer of sliced mozzarella and a layer of the tomato sauce. Continue layering in this order until all the ingredients are used up, ending with a sauce layer (this will keep the dish moist – if you want a crisp top, end with aubergine and Parmesan).

Bake in the oven at 180°C (350°F) Gas 4 for 30–35 minutes until browned and bubbling. Remove and set aside for 10 minutes to settle before serving. Serve warm or at room temperature.

imam bayildi

4 large aubergines, with long stalks if possible, halved lengthways

200 ml extra virgin olive oil

500 g onions, halved and very thinly sliced

4 garlic cloves, crushed

750 g plum tomatoes, skinned, deseeded and finely chopped

leaves from 15 sprigs of flat leaf parsley

leaves from 12 sprigs of marjoram

2 teaspoons sugar

1 small lemon, thinly sliced

sea salt and freshly ground black pepper

an ovenproof dish, big enough to hold the aubergine in a single layer

serves 4–8

carbohydrate 25 g

The story goes that this dish got its name because the priest (the Imam) found it so delicious that he swooned. Some stories tell that he fainted because he was horrified at the amount of oil used to cook it. This is the secret – aubergines must be cooked well, with large quantities of oil. This recipe uses scented marjoram (when it has its flowers in bloom, use those, too) and lots of parsley.

Cut a line 5 mm in from the edges of the aubergine halves, then score the flesh inside with a criss-cross pattern. Rub plenty of oil all over the aubergines and season with a little salt. Arrange in a single layer in the ovenproof dish. Cook in a preheated oven at 200°C (400°F) Gas 6 for about 30 minutes or until the flesh has just softened.

Heat 75 ml of the oil in a heavy-based frying pan, add the onions and garlic, cover with a lid and cook over low heat until soft. Increase the heat and add the tomatoes. Cook until the juices from the tomatoes have reduced a little, then add salt and pepper to taste. Reserve a few parsley leaves for serving, then chop the remainder together with the marjoram. Add to the onion and tomato mixture, then add the sugar.

Scoop some of the central flesh out of the aubergines, leaving a shell around the outside to hold the base in shape. Chop the scooped out section and add to the tomato mixture. Pile the mixture into the aubergine shells and sprinkle with pepper. Arrange the lemon slices on top. Trail more oil generously over the top, then sprinkle with 4 tablespoons of water.

Cover with foil and bake for 30–40 minutes until meltingly soft. Remove the foil about 10 minutes before the end. Serve, sprinkled with any remaining oil and the reserved parsley.

The secret of cooking cauliflower is to blanch it first, and if you add a bay leaf, the unpleasant cabbage aroma disappears. This gratin can be enjoyed on its own or as an accompaniment to roast lamb or pork, such as Slow-roasted Pork Loin with Rosemary, Madeira and Orange (page 174).

cauliflower gratin

1 fresh bay leaf

1 large cauliflower, separated into large florets

500 ml double cream

2 teaspoons Dijon mustard

160 g finely grated Comté cheese*

sea salt

a baking dish, about 25 cm diameter, greased with butter

serves 4–6

carbohydrate 11 g

Bring a large saucepan of water to the boil, add the bay leaf, salt generously, then add the cauliflower. Cook until still slightly firm, about 10 minutes. Drain and set aside.

Put the cream in a saucepan and bring to the boil. Boil for 10 minutes, then stir in the mustard and 1 teaspoon salt.

Divide the cauliflower into smaller florets, then stir into the cream sauce. Transfer to the prepared dish and sprinkle the cheese over the top in an even layer. Bake in a preheated oven at 200°C (400°F) Gas 6 until golden, about 40–45 minutes. Serve hot.

*Note Like Gruyère, Comté is a mountain cheese – from the Franche-Comté region to be precise – but the similarity stops there. Comté's distinct flavour comes from the milk used in the making, so the flavour varies with the seasons. A springtime diet of tender young shoots delivers milk that is very different from its winter counterpart, when the cows are nourished mainly on hay. Comté is darker in colour and fruitier in summer, paler and more nutty in winter. Use Emmental or Cantal if it is unavailable.

Onions contain natural antibiotics and are also low-GI. These onions should be served in their skins and the centres squeezed or spooned out by the guests. Serve as a starter or alternatively serve with roast lamb and insert a sprig of rosemary into the onions before roasting.

roast onions
with herbed butter

12 large red onions
4 tablespoons olive oil
sea salt and freshly ground black pepper

herbed butter

250 g unsalted butter, softened
4 tablespoons chopped fresh herbs, such as thyme, tarragon and/or chives

serves 6

carbohydrate 38 g

To make the herbed butter, put the butter in a bowl and mash with a fork. Add the herbs and mash again. Use from the bowl, or chill a little, transfer to a sheet of kitchen foil and roll into a log. The log may be kept in the refrigerator or frozen for future use. You can cut off rounds to use with dishes such as pan-grilled steak or steamed vegetables.

Leaving the skins on, take a small slice off each onion root and trim the ends so they will sit upright. Brush them all over with half the olive oil and cut each one from the top down towards the root without cutting right through. Give them a quarter turn and make a similar cut as before.

Pack them closely into a roasting tin so they sit upright. Open the cuts a little, pour ½ teaspoon of oil into each one, then sprinkle with salt and pepper.

Roast in a preheated oven at 190°C (375°F) Gas 5 for 1½ hours or until the centres are soft. Lift them onto individual plates and put a spoonful of herb butter into each one.

Variation Put 4 tablespoons cider vinegar, 4 tablespoons honey, 2 crushed garlic cloves and 1 tablespoon raisins in a saucepan and simmer for 1 minute. Add this to the onions during the last 30 minutes of cooking time.

Garlic has many health benefits and can be eaten raw or cooked, when it mellows and sweetens. You might think that whole roast heads of garlic would taste a bit robust, but such long cooking renders the cloves soft and nutty. Press out the flesh and spread it on toast, then serve in soups, with stews, or with this summery salad.

roast whole heads of garlic
with goats' cheese

4 whole heads of garlic

olive oil, plus extra to serve

sea salt and freshly ground black pepper

to serve

bitter leaves, such as frisée, or peppery ones, such as rocket

8 slices goats' cheese, about 2 cm thick

lemon wedges

8 oven-toasted slices of French bread, about 2.5 cm wide, or 16 small slices melba toast

serves 8

carbohydrate 27 g

Cut each head of garlic in half, then arrange in a single layer in a roasting tin. Spoon olive oil over the top and sprinkle with salt. Roast in a preheated oven at 200°C (400°F) Gas 6 for 45 minutes–1 hour or until the cloves are very soft.

Serve on a bed of bitter leaves with a thick slice of goats' cheese and a wedge of lemon. Dress with olive oil and black pepper. Guests press the garlic paste out of the papery peel and spread it on the toasts. Eat with the cheese and salad leaves.

Variations Individually roast garlic cloves Arrange the peeled garlic cloves in an ovenproof dish, add 4 tablespoons olive oil and toss until well coated. Roast in a preheated oven at 180°C (350°F) Gas 4 for 30 minutes.

Roast garlic with sugar and brandy Roast peeled garlic cloves as above for 30 minutes, then sprinkle with 4 tablespoons sugar and 4 tablespoons brandy. Return to the oven for another 30 minutes until they are crunchy.

grilled and sautéed mushrooms

4 large portobello mushrooms or 4 large fresh porcini mushrooms

3 tablespoons olive oil, plus extra for brushing

200 ml white wine

2 garlic cloves, chopped

freshly squeezed juice of 1 lemon

3 tablespoons chopped fresh parsley

sea salt and freshly ground black pepper

serves 4

carbohydrate 1 g

Combined with olive oil, garlic and parsley, these mushrooms make a great vegetarian starter or light lunch, or they could accompany a plainly grilled steak, such as Beefsteak with Rocket (page 162). The alcohol in the wine is cooked off in the reduction, but the wine adds a delicious flavour.

Pull the stalks off the mushrooms and set the caps gill side up on an oiled grill pan. Chop the stalks finely and set aside. Brush the mushrooms with olive oil, season with salt and pepper and cook under a preheated grill for 5 minutes.

Meanwhile, put 3 tablespoons olive oil in a frying pan with the white wine, garlic, lemon juice, parsley and the reserved chopped mushroom stalks. Bring to the boil, then boil hard to reduce by half. Season well and take off the heat. Transfer the mushrooms to warm serving plates and pour the sauce over the top. Serve immediately.

There are so many wild and cultivated mushrooms available now that it seems a pity not to take advantage of them in stir-fries, where their form, colour and flavour are shown off to best advantage. A wonderful mixture is cooked here with the famous 'Chinese trinity' of stir-fry tastes – aromatic garlic, ginger and spring onions.

chinese mushrooms
with spring onions and sesame seeds

1 kg assorted mushrooms, such as shiitakes, enokitakes, or yellow or pink oyster mushrooms (but not grey)

2 tablespoons groundnut oil

2 garlic cloves, crushed

3 cm fresh ginger, peeled and grated or thinly sliced

6 spring onions, thinly sliced

1 teaspoon sugar

2 teaspoons soy sauce

2 tablespoons toasted sesame seeds (page 52)

serves 4

carbohydrate 2 g

To prepare the mushrooms, remove the stems from the shiitakes and cut the caps in half. Slice off the end of the roots from the enokitakes and break the clumps into sections. Trim off the cut end of the roots from all the other mushrooms and brush the caps clean with a soft cloth. Leave the oyster mushrooms whole and slice the rest in half lengthways.

Heat the oil in a wok, add the garlic, ginger and spring onions and stir-fry for about 20 seconds. Add the firmer kinds of mushrooms and stir-fry for a few minutes.

Add the sugar and soy sauce and stir-fry quickly until the sugar has been dissolved. Add the oyster and enokitake mushrooms, turning gently in the sauce without breaking them up. Transfer to a serving plate, sprinkle with the sesame seeds and serve immediately with a meat dish.

Arguably the best-tasting squash, butternut squash is a good alternative to potato and an ideal accompaniment to many dishes such as Rolled Turkey Breast with Spinach, Bacon and Cheese (page 155), or casseroles and braises. If you roast it at a high heat it will brown, and if cooked more gently, it marries well with fresh herbs.

roast butternut squash
with garlic and thyme

1 large butternut squash or 2 small ones

2 tablespoons olive oil

6 tablespoons unsalted butter

a bunch of fresh thyme, tips snipped into sprigs

2 garlic cloves, sliced

sea salt and freshly ground black pepper

serves 4–8

carbohydrate 21 g

Cut the squash in half lengthwise and scoop out the seeds and pith with a spoon. Cut each half into 3–4 wedges, according to the size of the squash. There is no need to peel them.

Put the oil and butter in a roasting pan and heat on top of the stove until melted. Add the wedges of butternut and baste the pieces, turning them carefully to cover. Push the sprigs of thyme and slices of garlic between the wedges and sprinkle with salt and pepper.

Roast in a preheated oven at 190°C (375°F) Gas 5 for 30 minutes, turning the pieces over several times to brown them lightly.

Variation Peel the wedges of butternut with a vegetable peeler or turning knife. Bring a large saucepan of salted water to a boil, add the wedges, return to the boil and simmer for about 5 minutes. Drain well. This initial parboiling seasons them with salt to bring out their flavour and also gives a crunchy exterior.

A cooling summer dish, it looks and tastes sunny and fresh. It's ideal for a summer party or barbecue – you can prepare and cook it before your guests arrive, then leave it to soak up the oil, mint and balsamic vinegar. Serve with grilled or barbecued food, such as chicken or lamb.

courgettes and patty pans
infused with mint and balsamic vinegar

400 g yellow and green patty pans, halved

6 tablespoons olive oil

2 tablespoons balsamic vinegar

40 g pine nuts, lightly toasted in a dry frying pan

a handful of fresh mint leaves, coarsely chopped

3 courgettes (about 500 g), cut lengthways into 5 mm slices

sea salt and freshly ground black pepper

a ridged stove-top grill pan

serves 4

carbohydrate 15 g

Put the patty pans on a preheated barbecue or a ridged stove-top grill pan. Cook on each side for about 5 minutes or until tender, turning over when starting to char.

When cooked, transfer to a long serving dish. Pour over the oil and vinegar and sprinkle with pine nuts, mint, salt and pepper.

Cook the sliced courgettes on the barbecue or in the pan for just 1–2 minutes each side. Add to the patty pan mixture, turn to coat, cover and let marinate for about 2 hours in the refrigerator, then serve.

Note Patty pans are members of the squash family and are either yellow or green. They look a little alien, rather like mini flying saucers, but taste wonderful. They are available from large supermarkets all summer.

Poor old celery; it is more often an ingredient than the star of a dish. However, here it takes centre stage. Beef is the ideal complement to the trinity of celery, tomatoes and anchovies, so serve this with roast beef or grilled steaks, such as Rib Eye Steak with Anchovy Butter (page 164).

braised celery
with lardons and anchovies

2 whole bunches of celery

2 tablespoons extra virgin olive oil

75 g bacon lardons

1 onion, halved, then quartered and sliced

1 carrot, halved lengthways, then quartered and sliced

2 garlic cloves, sliced

200 g canned chopped tomatoes

250 ml dry white wine

1 fresh bay leaf

50 g canned anchovy fillets, about 8, drained and chopped

a handful of fresh flat leaf parsley, chopped

sea salt and freshly ground black pepper

serves 4-6

carbohydrate7 g

Remove any tough outer stalks from the celery and trim the tips so they will just fit into a large sauté pan with a lid.

Bring a large saucepan of water to the boil. Add a pinch of salt, then the celery and simmer gently for 10 minutes to blanch. Remove, drain and pat dry with kitchen paper.

Heat the oil in the sauté pan. Add the bacon lardons, onion and carrot and cook gently until lightly browned. Add the celery and a little salt and pepper and cook just to brown, then remove.

Add the garlic, cook for 1 minute, then add the tomatoes, wine and bay leaf. Bring to the boil and cook for 1 minute. Add the celery, cover and simmer gently for 30 minutes, turning the celery once during cooking.

Transfer the celery to a serving dish. Raise the heat and cook the sauce to reduce it slightly, about 10 minutes. Pour it over the celery, sprinkle with the anchovies and parsley and serve.

purple sprouting broccoli
with lemon and parmesan

Broccoli is one of those vegetables you either love or hate. One reason may be that it is difficult to cook well – over-boiling and blandness are common afflictions. This recipe should remedy both and it might even make a few broccoli converts along the way.

600 g purple sprouting or tenderstem broccoli

6 tablespoons extra virgin olive oil

freshly squeezed juice of 1 lemon

2–3 tablespoons freshly grated Parmesan cheese

sea salt

serves 4

carbohydrate 4 g

Bring a large saucepan of water to the boil, add salt, then add the broccoli. Blanch 1–2 minutes, then drain and refresh under cold running water. Drain in a colander, then pat dry thoroughly with kitchen paper.

Working in two batches, heat 3 tablespoons of the oil in a large non-stick pan. Add the broccoli (it should fit in a single layer so it browns evenly). Cook on high heat for 1–2 minutes, resisting the urge to stir, so that the broccoli gets nicely browned (but not burnt). Stir, then leave to brown on the other side, about 1–2 minutes more. Squeeze ½ lemon over the broccoli and cook, stirring for about 30 seconds. Transfer to a dish, season with salt, then add half the Parmesan. Toss well. Repeat with the remaining broccoli. Serve hot or at room temperature.

Variation You could add a chopped red chilli when cooking the second batch, if you like things hot.

The joy of this dish is that you need not stick to the same selection of vegetables as here. Mushrooms and red onions also roast well in a medley and you can also ring the changes with different herbs and spices. An endlessly adaptable dish.

roast summer vegetables

1 small aubergine, or
3–4 Japanese aubergines

4 small red onions

1 sweet potato

3 tablespoons olive oil

8 cherry tomatoes

2 red or yellow peppers

2 medium courgettes or 1 small
soft-skinned squash

1 whole head of garlic,
separated into cloves,
but unpeeled

1–2 large sprigs of rosemary
or thyme

sea salt

serves 4

carbohydrate 31 g

Slice the aubergine into bite-sized wedges, quarter the onions, peel the sweet potato and cut it into chunks.

Put the aubergine, onions and sweet potato in a plastic bag, add the oil and shake gently until everything is well coated. Transfer them all to a roasting tin and sprinkle with salt. Add the tomatoes and turn to coat with the oil.

Roast in a preheated oven at 230°C (450°F) Gas 8 for 15 minutes while you prepare the other vegetables.

Remove the stalks from the peppers and the seeds and ribs from the inside. Slice the flesh into thick wedges or chunks. Trim the courgettes and cut them lengthways into quarters and again in half if they are too long. If using squash, deseed and cut into chunks.

Add the peppers and courgettes to the roasting tin, turning them all in the oil. Tuck in the garlic and rosemary and return the tin to the oven for another 15 minutes. Lower the oven temperature to 180°C (350°F) Gas 4 and cover the tin with foil. Remove the foil after 15 minutes. If there is too much liquid in the tin, continue roasting uncovered for a final 10 minutes or so.

Serve as an accompaniment to roast meats or with other dishes as a light lunch.

sweet things and drinks

strawberries and cherries
in tricolour chocolate

250 g strawberries, stalks on

250 g cherries, stalks on

30 g milk chocolate, broken into small pieces

30 g white chocolate, broken into small pieces

30 g dark chocolate, broken into small pieces

greaseproof paper

mini muffin paper cases

serves 4

carbohydrate 16 g

Strawberries are an excellent source of vitamin C and their sweet softness combines well with the firmness of cherries. These chocolate treats can be prepared well in advance of serving and make a truly seductive end to any dinner party.

Divide the strawberries and cherries into 3 equal piles.

Put the milk chocolate into a clean, dry, heatproof bowl and set over a saucepan of gently simmering water.

Do not let the water touch the base of the bowl, or any water touch the chocolate, or the chocolate will seize and be unusable.

Take one of the piles of fruit and dip them halfway into the chocolate, leaving the tops and stalks uncoated and visible. Transfer to a sheet of greaseproof paper to set.

Repeat with the white and dark chocolate and the other two piles of fruit. Chill for at least 1 hour.

To serve, peel off the greaseproof paper and put a selection of fruit in a mini muffin case. Alternatively, pile the fruit onto a large serving plate and invite your guests to help themselves.

Note You must use a clean, dry bowl for each kind of chocolate, or the chocolate will be spoiled.

strawberries
with black pepper

500 g strawberries
1 tablespoon orange flower water (optional)
1 tablespoon caster sugar
2 teaspoons freshly ground black pepper

serves 4

carbohydrate 11 g

Strawberries and black pepper are surprisingly good partners. Orange flower water adds a lovely perfumed quality to the strawberries.

Hull the strawberries and cut in half. Sprinkle with the orange flower water, if using, and with the sugar and black pepper. Chill for 15 minutes and serve.

Note Strawberries should be washed and dried before hulling, not after, otherwise they fill up with water.

rhubarb compote
with yoghurt

500 g rhubarb, trimmed
50 g caster sugar, or to taste
125 g natural yoghurt
1 tablespoon clear honey
½ tablespoon rosewater

serves 4

carbohydrate 19 g

Rhubarb is a good low-carb food. Once cooked, the compote can be kept in the fridge for a few hours until ready to serve with the yoghurt.

Cut the rhubarb into 5-cm slices and put into a saucepan. Add the caster sugar and 4 tablespoons water. Bring to the boil, cover and simmer gently for 15 minutes until the rhubarb has softened. Transfer to a dish and let cool.

Put the yoghurt, honey and rosewater into a bowl, mix well, then serve with the rhubarb.

350 g ricotta cheese,
at room temperature

350 g mascarpone cheese,
at room temperature

1 tablespoon dark rum

3 tablespoons Tia Maria,
Kahlúa or other coffee liqueur

1 teaspoon vanilla essence

4 tablespoons icing sugar,
or to taste

2 tablespoons finely ground
espresso Italian roast coffee

grated dark chocolate, to
decorate (optional)

6–8 tiny cups of hot espresso
coffee, to serve

*6–8 flexible ice cream moulds or
small ramekins*

serves 8

carbohydrate 8 g

A semifreddo is a pudding that is half frozen to give it a slightly thickened, creamy texture. Sometimes it is made of whipped cream lightened with meringue, then flavoured with anything from vanilla to passionfruit. In this example, the espresso gives an interesting texture, but you must buy it very finely ground. Both ricotta and mascarpone cheese are low-carb foods.

coffee semifreddo with espresso

Put the ricotta and mascarpone in a bowl, and beat with a wooden spoon. (Do not attempt to do this in a food processor or the mixture will be too runny.) Beat in the rum, Tia Maria, vanilla essence and icing sugar. Fold in the ground espresso so that the mixture is marbled. Carefully spoon into the ice cream moulds or ramekins, piling the mixture high. Freeze for 2 hours.

Transfer to the refrigerator 15–20 minutes before serving to soften slightly. The mixture should be only just frozen or very chilled. Just before serving, dip the moulds quickly in warm water and invert into chilled shallow bowls. Decorate with a little grated chocolate, if using, then serve immediately with tiny cups of espresso for guests to pour over the semifreddo.

Wrapping fruits in foil is a great way to cook them in the oven or on the barbecue – all the juices are contained in the parcel while the fruit softens, and the aroma when you open the parcel will make your mouth water. Buy the fruits in season for the best flavour.

baked fruit parcels

4 peaches or nectarines, halved, stoned and sliced

100 g blueberries

100 g raspberries

freshly squeezed juice of 1 orange

1 teaspoon ground cinnamon

1 tablespoon caster sugar

150 g Greek yoghurt

2 teaspoons clear honey

1 tablespoon rosewater

1 tablespoon chopped pistachio nuts

serves 4

carbohydrate 23 g

Put the fruit into a large bowl, add the orange juice, cinnamon and sugar and mix well. Divide the fruit mixture among 4 sheets of foil. Fold the foil over the fruit and seal the edges to make parcels.

Put the yoghurt, honey and rosewater into a separate bowl and mix well. Set aside until required.

Cook the parcels in a preheated oven at 220°C (425°F) Gas 7 for 5–6 minutes. Alternatively, preheat a barbecue, then cook the parcels over medium hot coals.

Remove the parcels from the heat, open carefully and transfer to 4 serving bowls. Serve with the yoghurt and a sprinkling of pistachio nuts.

As well as being delicious, raspberries are one of the best fruit sources of fibre. Unsweetened soya milk is a lower carb alternative to dairy milk, but choose a fortified version to ensure you don't miss out on calcium. You may find it doesn't need a sweetener – but if your sweet tooth is incurable, add a little honey (but remember, each teaspoon of honey adds around 6 g carbohydrate).

raspberry smoothie
with soya milk

1 punnet raspberries, about 150 g

about 500 ml unsweetened soya milk

12 ice cubes

honey, to taste (optional)

serves 4

carbohydrate 3 g

Put the raspberries*, soya milk and ice cubes in a blender and purée to a froth. Serve the honey separately so people can sweeten to taste.

*Note If you love raspberries, reserve a few and sprinkle on top of each glass before serving.

12 ice cubes

4 scoops strawberry ice cream

12 large ripe strawberries,
hulled and halved

125 ml low-fat yoghurt

125 ml low-fat milk

serves 4

carbohydrate 21 g

Strawberry smoothies are invariably the most popular with guests. Serve them made just with ice, or with yoghurt, ice cream or milk. Or, as here, with the lot – we can all be a little self-indulgent once in a while.

strawberry ice cream smoothie

Put the ice cubes in a blender and blend to a snow. Add the ice cream, strawberries and yoghurt and blend again, adding enough milk to give a creamy consistency. Pour into glasses and serve.

blueberry and orange smoothie

freshly squeezed juice of
4 oranges

half a punnet blueberries,
about 250 g

sparkling mineral water, to taste

serves 2

carbohydrate 25 g

Vitamin C is vital for life, and fresh fruits and juice are the best ways of getting it, especially oranges and blueberries. Commercial juices are often pasteurized or heat-treated to sterilize and preserve them. Heat destroys vitamin C, so manufacturers replace it in the form of ascorbic acid.

Put the orange juice in a blender, add the blueberries and blend until smooth. Alternatively, peel the oranges, then feed half of them through a juicer, followed by the blueberries, then the remaining oranges.

Add mineral water to taste and serve.

berry, apricot and orange slush

4 ripe apricots, halved and
pitted, then coarsely chopped

8 strawberries, hulled
and halved

freshly squeezed juice of
1 orange

sparkling mineral water,
to taste

serves 1

carbohydrate 25 g

Orange juice will help to extend more expensive fruits, and their gentle acidity also develops the flavour. Apricots are very dense, so you may like to pulp them in the blender rather than putting them through the juicer. If you do decide to juice, remove the skins* first, and juice them alternately with pieces of apple.

Put the apricots, strawberries and orange juice in a blender and purée until smooth, adding mineral water to taste. (If the mixture is too thick, add a few ice cubes and blend again.)

Note To remove the apricot skins, bring a saucepan of water to the boil, then blanch the apricots for about 1 minute. Remove the skin with the back of a knife.

The wonderful thing about this smoothie is that you can change the colour depending on which fruits you choose. Berries are lower in carbohydrate than most fruits. This nutritious smoothie makes a filling and nutritious breakfast drink or, alternatively, a healthy low-carb snack to stave off hunger between meals.

red berry smoothie

1 punnet berries (about 250 g), such as strawberries, cranberries, redcurrants or raspberries (for a pink smoothie) or blackberries and blueberries (for a blue smoothie)

250 ml natural yoghurt

125 ml crushed ice

honey, to taste (optional)

serves 2–3

carbohydrate 17 g

Put all the berries, yoghurt and ice into a blender and work to a thin, frothy cream. If too thick, add a little water to create a pourable consistency.

Taste, then add honey if you prefer (but remember that this will increase the carbohydrate content).

Fennel can be very difficult to juice – you need a strong machine. Alternatively, chop it and purée in a blender with apple juice, then strain. Use a crisp, sweet, red apple, such as Red Delicious, to give a wonderful pinkish tinge. Always remove the stem and stalk ends of apples and pears, where any pesticides and residues collect.

apple juice
with fennel

1 fennel bulb, including sprigs of the feathery leaves

2 apples, cored but not peeled

juice of ½ lemon (optional)

serves 2

carbohydrate 13 g

Trim the green leaves from the fennel bulb, trim off the root end, then slice the bulb into long wedges and cut out and remove the cores from each wedge. Cut the apples into wedges. Put the apples and fennel through a juicer.

Stir in the lemon juice to prevent the discoloration of the apples and fennel, then serve immediately, topped with a few fennel sprigs for extra aroma.

bloody mary

250 ml vodka

500 ml tomato juice

3½–4 tablespoons lemon juice

½ teaspoon Tabasco, or to taste

1 teaspoon Worcestershire
sauce, or to taste

a pinch of freshly ground
white pepper

to serve

ice cubes

4 celery sticks

few celery leaves, finely
chopped (optional)

serves 4

carbohydrate 4 g

Although there are chilli sauces the world over, none is as instantly recognizable as Tabasco, from Avery Island in Louisiana, where it has been produced since 1868. A mixture of 'tabasco' (supposedly pequín) chillies, vinegar and salt, the sauce is aged in oak barrels. Here it's used to spice up a mixture of tomato juice, vodka and lemon juice, with a celery stick to stir it all around. This is traditionally served at a brunch.

Put all the ingredients in a blender, pulse to mix to a smooth consistency, then pour into 4 medium-size glasses half-filled with ice cubes. Alternatively, put the ingredients in a cocktail shaker, add ice and shake. Strain into 4 medium-size glasses half-filled with ice cubes.

Add a celery stick and a few chopped celery leaves, if using, to each glass, then serve.

index

photography credits